The Lonely Teacher

PETER KNOBLOCK

and

ARNOLD P. GOLDSTEIN

Syracuse University

ALLYN AND BACON, INC.
Boston

To
Marion and Joe
and
Herman and Rose

Library of Congress Catalog Card Number: 73–151969

Contents

66821

Preface

In this book we attempt to capture the perceptions of a group of teachers reporting the quality of their interpersonal relationships with children. A small-group process approach was developed in which these teachers explore their feelings, concerns, and interactions with children and with other school staff members.

The book is divided into four parts and includes an Appendix. Part I explores the theme of teacher loneliness. The interpersonal and organizational conditions giving rise to feelings of aloneness are discussed. Part II discusses the utilization of group approaches to facilitate communication between staff members. Part III contains a description of the actual group process in which these teachers participated. An analysis of the process is made by focusing on group concepts such as leadership, cohesiveness, and phase movement. Part IV analyzes the quality of individual teacher-pupil relationships. The Appendix reports findings obtained from the "Teacher-Pupil Relationship Inventory" as completed by each teacher, her pupils, and by each group member.

In education we are experiencing a resurgence of interest in the impact of schooling on children. Much is being written maintaining that educators and schools need to consider and take into account what is going on in the heads and hearts of schoolchildren. We, too, are concerned about the children, and in this book we look at the interactional dynamics between children and their teachers. Mostly, we asked our group of teachers to allow us access to their feelings and concerns about themselves and their functioning with children.

We feel privileged to have been a part of this very beautiful experience in which teachers shared their interpersonal and personal joys and griefs with us and the group members. Every attempt has been made to remain as close to the statements of teachers as is possible. Hopefully, our analyses and attempts to conceptualize the group process and interactional concerns have not detracted from the humanness of the teachers' actual words and concerns.

Despite the fact that this was a group of teachers of troubled children functioning within the framework of Special Education, it is our belief that the feelings of loneliness and the deep concerns that teachers have for human contact with other adults as well as with children are universal concerns of all teachers. These concerns, in our experience, do not seem unique to one group of teachers in one type of school. They are human relations concerns surfacing within an organizational structure known as "school," and schools have not always made a clear commitment to the personal growth of teachers and children.

To think back to those who made this book possible and to find adequate ways to thank them reminds us again of the many persons we came to know and respect. Certainly, we wish to thank the participating group of teachers for their initial willingness to take part in the group meetings and for their openness in responding. If anything, we should all take comfort in being witness to the incredible humanness of those who spend time with our children. More and more teachers, we believe, can be brought closer to who they are with children and to recognize their feelings provided they have an opportunity to explore such terrain.

Our gratitude goes to many of our colleagues who read and shared their reactions with us—particularly, Ralph A. Garcea, whose insights and experiences in schools and with groups of teachers form a significant portion of this book. Finally, we thank Janyce Reiman and Mary Kishman for their competent assistance in the typing and preparation of this manuscript.

Introduction

The project reported in this book began with what seemed to be a very limited goal—that of gaining a clearer understanding of what *really* transpires when teachers and children interact. We wanted to bring ourselves much closer to whatever it is they do with and to each other. In preparing an earlier statement on teacher-pupil relationships it became apparent that little has been written which focuses directly on human communications in classrooms. (See Knoblock, P., and Garcea, R. A. Teacher-child relationships in psycho-educational programming for emotionally disturbed children, *Educational therapy*, Vol. 2, Seattle, Wash.: Special Child Publications, 1969.) Efforts to capture the transactional qualities of these daily encounters have been hampered by a kind of booming, buzzing confusion taking form in literally thousands of interpersonal contacts each day between a given teacher and his pupils. As we push forward to our search for a scientific basis to understanding classroom dynamics we have turned toward the development of classroom observational instruments. In many ways, such instruments have helped considerably, primarily as they have influenced and legitimized the entry into classrooms of professional workers other than teachers. In other ways, however, classroom interaction instruments have been more useful in providing us with information regarding the frequency of various types of classroom interactions rather than their quality and intensity.

Much of the basis for the development of a small group process approach involving teachers is our belief that teachers' perceptions and relationships with others should be the units of study. Whatever preciseness may be lost by focusing on what it is that teachers say and feel in contrast to objectively measuring it, other benefits may accrue by such an approach, primarily in capturing the extent of their affect and concern. To be sure, in order to some day complete our under-

1

standing of teacher-pupil relationships, rigor in the form of objective data collection will be needed along with the more visceral reactions of those teachers who face children and themselves each day. But for the present it would seem we are very far from objectifying what occurs between teachers and their pupils. Results from many classroom interaction studies rather consistently point out how direct teachers are in their communications with pupils. Such teacher directness often takes the form of lecturing, giving directions, criticizing or justifying authority. It would be a serious mistake to accept such findings without raising the major question of "Is that how teachers really want to behave?"

This project was begun in an attempt to obtain information as to the kinds of teacher-pupil relationships which were experienced by six teachers of small groups of children labelled disturbed and disturbing. Four of the six teachers had received their graduate training in the same preparation program, although not all at the same time. All had received training in special education and, in addition to their current employment with difficult children, three had prior experience in regular elementary education. Their range of teaching experience was from one to five years. Each teacher was contacted individually and told of our interest in exploring the dynamics of teacher-pupil relationships with a small group of teachers.

Part I discusses the feelings of aloneness described by this group of teachers. It is our feeling that what they expressed and experienced could be replicated by many teachers and many teacher groups. It became quite clear that only some of their concerns about what they felt and how they responded centered around their contacts with children. A fair amount of time, their concern had to do with adult relationships in the school and community.

Part II begins with a brief review of literature which describes teachers functioning in groups. The remainder of that section looks at the various purposes and functions group process approaches may serve for teachers.

A decision was made by the authors to develop a group flexibility but at the same time to provide a way of focusing on the phases of group development. The broad task of the group was to focus on teacher-pupil relationships.

Part III discusses a three-phase group development which grew out of the authors' beliefs as to how a group could be assisted to focus on the personal and interpersonal qualities of teacher-pupil interactions. In the first phase the focus was on specific problem children and could be considered the *Pupil Centered Phase*. The second phase, a *Teacher-Pupil Relationship Phase*, was an attempt to move away from a strict focus on the problems of the child to the interactional problems of the teacher and child. The third phase was labelled *New Problem Solving*, with the goal being that of generalizing from the insights learned in this group to other pupils and teachers and to other group situations, hopefully to the classrooms and schools in which they were involved.

It is conceivable that we began this project looking for answers as to what constitutes teacher-pupil relationships. Before very long, however, it was patently clear that the group *process* we were all engaged in was far more potent than the *product*, particularly in view of the fact that we had very imprecise notions of the product we were looking for regarding teacher-pupil relationships. The group process approach which was conceptualized and implemented is just one approach among many which could be utilized. If we can rely upon the clinical and suggested statistical support gathered from our project and reported in the remainder of this book, then it would seem that this and other group approaches with teachers could serve as an "unfreezing" process. It was our hope that by helping to create an atmosphere of trust and sharing, these teachers would be able and willing to communicate what their relationships with children looked like and what they hoped such relationships could become.

There is nothing magical about groups and the healing power such groups hold for many of the group members. When and if such groups accomplish the purposes for which they were designed, it is because all or a majority of those in the group have worked very hard to make the group function in a facilitative way. Part III will clearly highlight the pushes and pulls operating on the group members as they moved toward and away from the tasks we and the group members had set up. As an in-depth examination of the group's development and behavior, Part III strives to represent the group as it appeared to function. This focus is an attempt to keep our material as close to the teachers as possible, reporting accurately what it was that happened in the group and what it was that teachers said.

Part IV moves away from the focus on group life to the study of what it is that teachers have to say about their relationships with individual children. Again, there is a heavy reliance upon the actual words of the teachers as they express their successes and failures, joys and fears.

For those desiring a more quantitative evaluation of this project, the findings from psychological tests contained in the Appendix will be of interest. As commented upon earlier in this introduction, it would seem desirable to combine in some way qualitative and quantitative analysis of interpersonal relationships. We have attempted to develop instruments for exploring both the perceptions of interpersonal relationships held by teachers and their pupils and the perceptions held by each group member of others' interpersonal behavior and growth. We do wish to emphasize, however, that we consider our test data and interpretations strictly exploratory and tentative at this time.

Under no circumstances have we conceived of this book and the material contained herein as providing any final answers. In many ways we are rather excited at the potential good a group process approach can effect. This experience demonstrated to us how useful it can be for concerned teachers to share their feelings and perceptions with others in a group setting. It also became apparent that such a group design has applicability for a teacher's functioning in the classroom with children, and in the school with other adults. After all, our group members brought their in-school concerns to our meetings and experienced a process in which communication between persons was facilitated. Invariably the themes of our discussions had to do with human relations concerns "back there" in school. It is our belief that teachers experiencing a group process situation in which communication and understanding are enhanced will be a step closer to trying out their new learnings in their classrooms and schools.

I

The Lonely Teacher:
Feelings of Separateness

In the song "Eleanor Rigby," the Beatles ask where do all the lonely people come from. We now know that many of them must be in classrooms with children, wearing the same impersonal masks that leave an Eleanor Rigby one of society's dropouts. There had been no early decision to title this book *The Lonely Teacher*, but after experiencing our material we were struck with the realization that one of the core concerns teachers experienced was that of loneliness. For quite some time now education majors and new teachers have reported how far removed textbooks and college classrooms were from the realities of the public school classroom. Perhaps if we had been listening more carefully we could have discerned the message that powerful things happen to classroom teachers, something not captured by textbook writers and even the popular press. The "something" appears to be the gigantic struggle on the part of many teachers to facilitate the academic and personal growth of children against what is often characterized as overwhelming odds. The current educational scene is being placed before the American reading public by a group of writers, many of them teachers such as John Holt, Jonathan Kozol, Herbert Kohl and others. Such writers have been referred to as "romantics," perhaps because of the questing nature of what they are searching for in seeking to make education relevant for children. Many education critics and teacher-writers have expressed their anger at what they see; and what they report are school environments which throw up so many obstacles before teachers and children that a stifling of responses and creativity are the only results. It is also true that the number of attacks on schools is increasing in frequency and intensity. It is possible to ignore what is going on inside the heads of teachers while we focus so hard on what the external school environment is doing to children and teachers. This literature, which is being devoured by a critical American public, has done much to highlight the present barriers to whatever it is we consider sound education. By and large, the focus has been on the destructive nature of school climates and the impact on children. What our group of teachers had to say in our meetings makes clear that they too were suffering and buckling from the impact of harmful and even nonexistent school communication systems.

Basically, what our teachers and what many classroom teachers are experiencing is a rather painful realization that they are separate from themselves, their children, and other adults in school. They are casting about frantically trying to decipher very obtuse messages as to what are the goals and hopes of schools for children's learning and adjustment. Loneliness for teachers, it seems to us, comes in many sizes and shapes. It takes almost all of the forms we typically think of, and assumes some others of which we are just now becoming aware.

PHYSICAL AND PSYCHOLOGICAL SEPARATENESS

Certainly the physical isolation of teachers is a constant reminder to them of their separateness. The "classroom as a teacher's castle," while perhaps once serving as a useful fortification against ignorant outsiders (both school and community representatives), no longer seems justifiable. In the first place, it would seem that our efforts to educate educators, parents and the public as to what is happening in schools and also to sensitize them to the potential of educating for relevance has been quite successful. Many more people seem interested and involved in the education of their children, and for that matter in the education of teachers. While this increased interest has made for some clumsy encounters between "outsiders" and "insiders," the implication seems clear: that the openness of the schools is a goal being advanced by more citizens and by a growing number of educators.

One of the larger paradoxes regarding the classroom teacher and *his* classroom is that while the purpose of this environmental and psychological arrangement originally was to guarantee freedom to function, now it has all the potential of guaranteeing freedom to fail. As teachers become more vocal in their demands for both psychological and material support, relatively few outside of the classroom have a frame of reference for what goes on in the classrooms, and what teachers are in need of and why. It is doubly unfortunate that many of those not understanding teachers happen also to be educators—other teachers in the building, the principal—and the teacher next door!

For a number of reasons we are beginning to pay a rather high price for our "splendid isolation." For one thing, it is no longer as possible for teachers to control what others know about schools. What they need from others, in school and out, is now much more excessive that in asking for such assistance they in turn need to expose themselves in terms of their philosophy of teaching, their view of how children grow, indeed, if they see children growing, and how they implement their teaching strategies and stances.

It is precisely at this point that the confrontation occurs between a teacher's feeling of separateness and what that teacher needs to "give up" in order to be socially and professionally responsive to the school and community. A powerful factor contributing to this concern, and one which further contributes to this self-imposed teacher isolation, may be the monumental difficulty of the teaching task as they see it and as others expect them to behave. More than one teacher has indicated that they have all they can do to keep themselves together from day to day, much less venture out into the hall to see how anyone else is faring.

And as if it were not already extraordinarily complex enough, there is the large question raised by many teachers as to whether they should be responsive—even if they wanted to. Our group of teachers generally felt that the school organizational structure in which they were working was every bit as permeable and porous as they were. Faced with their own self doubts and needs for appropriate feedback and approval they were not at all certain there were external resources in the form of other school people who stood ready and able to be of assistance.

We are amazed at the number of anecdotes told by teachers that reflect their willingness to try reaching out *once* or *twice* to others in their school. Invariably what tends to happen is that these teachers sufficiently mask what kind of help they are asking for and those in the school who may respond do so in an equally clumsy manner. Perhaps the best, or worst, example are those instances in which a teacher expresses lack of knowledge of what to do with a particular child who is presenting a classroom management problem. Upon asking for advice, he gets it, sometimes with both barrels! We are reminded of the paper by Gibbs (1964) "Is Help Helpful?" Just because a teacher asks for advice doesn't mean he is laying himself open for evaluative comments by the responder. It may only take a few of these encounters to perpetuate the cycle of seclusiveness familiar to so many teachers. Somehow we need to develop our sensitivities in order to respond with alertness and compassion to those teachers who are willing to venture out into the school halls and teacher meetings and ask for help.

Based on what our group of teachers reported, there exists a fair amount of teacher confusion as to how to break this cycle of pessimism over how to ask for help, and whether it will be given once requested. There is a degree of truth to the anxieties teachers have over whether there are in fact others in the school who could and would support them. One of the more dramatic examples of this conscious pulling back is seen in the actions of a well-established special class program for children with learning and adjustment problems. After several years of trying to find a niche for themselves in several different public school buildings, they made the conscious decision to move their classes into the basement. Their justification was that they would have a degree of freedom to operate in their basement headquarters that would not be possible under the pressures and scrutiny of the rest of the school when situated on the first floor. By the time a situation has progressed as far as the above example indicates, it is too late to pinpoint the responsibility. In all likelihood, by the time there is such an advanced state of separateness all parties involved are acting out of self protection and defensiveness.

In our many contacts with teachers it has become apparent that we are also witnessing a self-imposed exile; a source of separateness has come about because teachers have simply not been aware of other alternatives. Having said this about teachers, note how analogous this is to how we describe difficult children's inflexible approaches to life situations. Considering how short-lived most teaching careers are, it is unlikely that most teachers have had an opportunity to experience themselves in a variety of teaching-learning environments. Our group of teachers reported how important it was to them to "fit" into the school and to do a "good job." The physical separation described above and limited alternatives seemingly apparent to teachers combined to exacerbate their feelings of loneliness.

Invariably what was described was a stumbling, halting kind of attempt by the teacher to "read" accurately what was acceptable teacher and child behavior in the school environment. Beyond the grossest observation that children's behavior needed to be *controlled*, whatever that means, most teachers are left to decipher all of the nuances of that message. At first glance the behavioral standards of a school seem crystal clear—no hitting of a teacher; no swearing; no running in the halls. But what about all the varieties of ways youngsters have of striking out at teachers—out of self defense, fury, uncontrolled anger, merely trying to squirm out of an adult's clutches and accidentally hitting, and so on? What if a teacher doesn't mind children swearing and even uses such language himself as a way of getting closer and responding with language familiar to and used by some children? Can children call a teacher by his first name, even if it doesn't happen in other classrooms?

This lack of clarity as to what is accepted and acceptable goes a long way toward compounding a teacher's feelings of isolation and separateness. The lack of alternatives possessed by teachers has propelled many of them into a frantic scramble for reading material which offers them such alternatives. Unfortunately, this has led to a proliferation of "how to do it" texts which ultimately leave all of us with the question we began with—who are we with children?

When one spends time in a public school it becomes apparent that there is a strong need on the part of many staff members to function according to a correct or appropriate set of behavioral expectations for children. As a goal this may be desirable, but its implementation in a school has frequently been oppressive. The implication for our group of teachers and for others is that deviancy in functioning as a teacher is more visible once such standards have been set. Rarely is the specification of norms very clear and articulate, but rather there develop more subtle standards that "everyone understands." While it is not true that everyone understands, it is just as true that very few teachers test the boundaries of what goes in their school. Such inaction is mostly a result of not having a process for sharing and communicating with other teachers.

A teacher who was actively ostracized by the other teachers on her grade level because of the type of classroom she was conducting stated that it made her feel better when she realized the others were really threatened by her competence and that it wasn't just that she was a poor teacher. A student teacher placed in her classroom said that what really frightened him was that others in the school disapproved of what his goals were for children rather than just his methods and techniques. In other words, what he said and what our group reported is that as soon as one affirms a more positive view of how children learn and develop social concerns for others it increases the risk of being labeled a deviant member of the school staff. Teachers report a climate of fear of novelty and jealousy over successes with children which lead to hoarding of ideas and materials. Most destructive of all could be the concern over sharing their fears and their inability to ask for the participation of other teachers and adults in the school in accomplishing goals for children.

We can see, then, the cycle of difficulty a teacher faces. The physical isolation of a teacher embodied in his having a classroom can also represent psychological isolation from others. Very often the lack of clear norms for the behavior of teachers with children can contribute to the rapid retreat of the teacher back into his classroom. We continue to be impressed with the human relations concerns that teachers have centered around other *adults*, not necessarily the children. Teachers of troubled children often report how necessary it is for them to find gratification and validation for their work in the responses given them by children, not other adults. They go on to indicate that this often becomes a burden under which many children cannot respond appropriately. After all, many children are experiencing rather demanding internal and external needs and are just not in a position to bolster a teacher's self-esteem. To whom does the teacher turn? We have many teachers, particularly new ones, tell us how both they and their spouses are figuratively going through the same job experience. With no one else to respond to their concerns, they take them home. More than one newly married teacher has told us *her husband* would refuse to let her take the job another year unless things get "better."

ADULT COMMUNICATION

For "things to get better" for teachers who are confronted with difficult children in their classrooms, there needs to be a reversal of teachers automatically internalizing their reactions of what they are doing to children and translating such feelings into negative self perceptions. Our group of teachers concluded that they must be bad persons for what they are doing and based this on the negative and minimal feedback they were receiving from other adults in the building. One of the more disastrous side-effects of not receiving open communications from other adults can be seen in the over-reliance of feedback from children.

Another frightening by-product of being isolated can be seen in the reports of teachers who maintain they are changing their belief systems regarding what they want to be for children. Paradoxical as it may seem, they maintain that being so much with children and understanding them so thoroughly in some ways turns them against children. Results of a followup study of graduates of a preparation program for teachers of difficult children indicated a dramatic shift from a child-centered focus when beginning teaching in a public school setting to a more teacher-centered focus after being there (Knoblock, Farrell, Lang, Sullivan, 1968). This finding is particularly troublesome in light of how difficult it has been for teachers to obtain very clear messages as to how they could and should and need to behave and what the reward system is in a school.

Clearly, then, there is a desperate, almost panicky need expressed by many teachers for clear communications with other adults. We have gone so far in extolling the virtues of a child-focused school that it borders on the unbelievable. No environment for children can accommodate to the needs for children's growth and development without an equal emphasis on an adult-centered process which also allows. for the continued growth of the adults—in this case the teachers and other school staff. Those involved in schools on a daily basis, particularly urban schools, cannot help being impressed with the constant barrage of stimuli faced by school staffs. It is day after day of coping with incidents and situations of a crisis nature that leaves such staffs with little time and energy for the long range curriculum planning and most importantly allows for little in the way of self-renewed activity by teachers.

One teacher, a warm and responsive young lady, indicated that she was seriously thinking of leaving teaching or at least only continuing her teaching career on a part time basis. Along with several personal concerns she felt that she was "too much with children," that she needed more adult contact. Another teacher walked into a noon-time meeting of college trainees and school staff and sat down explaining that she just needed to be with adults. If one wanted a barometer of the degree of loneliness and isolation from others that can exist in a school the lunch-time behavior of teachers would be one clue. In one elementary school such a "survey" was done only to find that with the exception of four or five teachers who always ate together, others scattered. Virtually all of the new teachers, or those experiencing difficulty managing the behavior in their classes were eating alone in their rooms. Only one or two would eat in the teachers' room. Just as distressing are those school staffs that do congregate in the teachers' room where the conversation is a mind-shattering resume of all that is wrong with schools, pupils, teachers, and life. It is all too often a quicksand bog of despair and bitching and while it may serve the purpose of catharsis for some, it is far too often a self perpetuation of the angriness and aloneness felt by so many teachers.

Before suggesting any solutions to effecting more helpful adult communication patterns in schools, if there are such solutions, perhaps we would do well to specify what it is that teachers feel they need to communicate and have communicated to them. In the *first* place, the "bad person" concern mentioned earlier is of paramount focus for many teachers. To overcome such a concern they are asking for sanctions for what they are doing and are seeking some one person or group with which to share very personal kinds of feelings, attitudes, and concerns they have about themselves as individuals who also happen to be teachers. It is so startling for us to realize that persons functioning as teachers are often no longer seen as individuals who have a past and a future, and least of all an inner life. There is a tendency on the part of many to infantilize teachers, to view them as doers of a task and nothing else. If something goes awry in a teacher's classroom, whatever that means, it is simply a matter of correcting whatever it is that is in front of us. We now know that many difficult children bring something to school that may prove to be a dynamic force in their interacting. It is just as reasonable to assume that not all of the teacher's behaviors are determined by the immediacy of the interaction with children. Faced with children's harsh reality life experiences, many of them carried to the school, we attempt to organize a planful environment which, while not always dealing directly with his problems, at least provides support in school for his strengths. Realizing the school's limited access to what goes on in children's (and adult's) lives outside of school, a reasonable approach would be to maximize the value of the in-school time, not as a curative, but as an environment in which teachers could maximize the skills they have and find an opportunity to capitalize on the resources of others, both children and teachers, and share with them their dreams of what learning environments could resemble.

Interpersonal needs and behaviors become circular, and unless the negative cycle is broken the harmful effects of perpetuation become rather immobilizing. One of the effects of infantilizing teachers, that is of refusing to respond to them as human beings with inner and outer experiences which shape their in-school behaviors, is to encourage their maintaining a dependent attitude on those perceived to be in authority. The frantic search for sanctioning of their behavior often grows out of a disbelief in oneself and a resultant search for outside support. It must be that such a "good job" has been done in the schools of establishing controls and checks and balances that relatively few teachers feel they have the power to operate independently. The harsh reality in most schools seems to be, however, that no one really wants to know what is going on. The less known and said the better.

Such applying of blinders is what is of concern to many teachers of difficult children. Those in our group and many other teachers are only in part intrigued with going their own way with children in their classrooms. They are fearful of becoming branded and identified as "deviant" such as their children have been labeled. One could argue, with as much justification as Kohl (1969) does, that it may be necessary to go one's own way in a school building. Our group of teachers, however, was holding tightly to teaching as part of an open communication system and hoped to effect some changes in their schools that would aid both them and their children.

Basic to their concerns was a need to somehow obtain validation for what they were doing and assistance in effecting changes. We were pleased to witness the degree of openness and even sacrificial quality of their asking for assistance. The destructive aspect of their time in school was that many of them did feel bad and hurtful. Just as with children, no learning or meaningful interaction can take place as long as people view themselves in such a way.

In the second place, our teachers wanted to communicate that they could represent themselves as complex individuals. To be sure, they wanted to do a good job in their classrooms with children, but they also felt they had good ideas about what could happen in schools with children and teachers. Even more importantly, they believed they had many skills and talents other than teaching skills. Many are talented and creative people who outside of the school pursue many avocations but within the school are asked to turn those off and run the ship as usual.

In a summer workshop dealing with interpersonal competence, a group of teachers began to discuss poetry. One of the participants began to bring her poems to class, some of them inspired by the workshop and its participants. Two things were startling about this experience. One was the very fact that such creative people and behavior were neither acknowledged nor provided for in their school jobs. The other was that their degree over animation of such "avocational interests" was far more intense and involving than their teaching activities in the classroom.

It would seem from what our group and other teachers report that it is not sufficient to develop a personal and professional life which focuses exclusively on children. Teachers are equally concerned with responding to other adults and in turn being responded to by their colleagues.

In short, teachers would like very much to function as resources within the schools. How paradoxical it is that so many teachers do not see themselves as resources within their own classrooms, but rather as keepers of the peace, curriculum and school tradition. It is this keeper role too that needs to be changed and some of our teachers felt such changes could be brought about if they were part of the school and not treated as foreign visitors.

THE VALUE OF INTERDEPENDENCE

For a number of reasons, some of them considered above, great numbers of teachers feel outside of the school in which they are working. It is just possible that a newer breed of teacher we have been preparing for is beginning to arrive, a teacher who cares about himself as a person and not just as a dispenser of society's accumulated wisdom and knowledge. A teacher who feels good enough about himself so that he comes to accept and acknowledge his own skills and creative talents which may or may not reflect the standard school curriculum. Eventually such people may even come to see themselves as change agents in their schools and not just placed in the position of reacting to other hostile adults and fending off the blows of loneliness.

Our group of teachers clearly pointed out that many factors led to their feelings of separateness and loneliness and that only some of them had to do with their work with children. They didn't know what successful teaching meant anymore. Some of them thought they knew when they began. It had something to do with caring for the child and focusing on his needs. Being a person for the child and developing that ever elusive thing called a relationship seemed to be at the heart of the matter, at least they thought it would be that way. They found that they were viewed, because of their commitment to self growth and children's growth as akin to missionaries, that is, with distrust and suspicion. No one seems to believe that for some teachers (and perhaps for more than we could ever imagine) their work with children is more than a job. We see now just how complex their need for "success" may be. For some it strikes at the very core of their need system—a need to feel competent and included in the teaching-learning community.

Many of them were appalled upon realizing that their deep feelings for the children were misperceived by other adults as highly improbable and very peculiar if one were to use the existing norms found in many schools—that of a clear separation of teacher from child. Many teachers, those in our group included, did not begin teaching with the intent of becoming an ombudsman for children, but that is what frequently developed. Often teachers who care for children are placed in the position of defending them. It is just a short step then until other staff members perceive such teachers and their children as having joined forces *against* the school and what it stands for! How devastating it is for some teachers to realize that they may be placed in the position of identifying with the child *or* with the school. Those who believe that schools are for the children are often disillusioned and frightened to be grouped with the children. That isn't what their caring was meant to do, but it is one of the outcomes. Once this happens and the battle lines are drawn, the lines of open communication are made even more difficult.

Concerned teachers are seeking positive reflections from adults, not just from children. Our group indicated that they gained a great deal of gratification from their work with children, but they expressed an equally strong need to share and communicate with other adults in the school. They felt frustrated and under pressure from other teachers, administrators, even pupils to behave as other respectable teachers, whatever that meant. This prior expectation was superimposed on them and it was their job to fit with such an expectation. It could amount to an endless foot race with the concerned teachers always trying to keep up with what seemed to be clear expectations held by other teachers, but which remained vague and elusive. The only clear notion was that classrooms are to be quiet places and few adults in a school wish to go beyond that.

This need to be fiercely independent may be an overdramatization of a once historical need, but if one listens closely to teachers there is a discernible interest in making adult as well as child contact. When spending time in schools and with teachers, it becomes quite clear that it is deception of the highest order not to believe that we are dealing with a small organizational structure which functions clandestinely if not allowed to surface. Even in schools with authoritarian principals who "clearly" spell out how children and teachers are to behave, his mandates are reworked and analyzed in dozens of faculty room encounters and after school phone calls. There are as many needs to be met by coming together as a group as there are teachers in a school. In one public school, teachers were encouraged to initiate items to be discussed at weekly faculty meetings. A small subgroup of teachers who identified themselves as the disciplinarians wanted the dress code for teachers clarified. At the meeting it became clear that there was no dress code and, even more importantly, teachers needed to decide for themselves what was appropriate dress. In short, individual freedoms were not to be legislated by others. In this instance a group of seemingly rigid teachers wanted a group focus if only to have their expectations met. Their interest was no less legitimate than that of other teachers with different sets of concerns. Some further examples might be of interest.

A subgroup of faculty from an elementary school, apparently feeling that there was not a place for their ideas in an open forum in the school, began to meet evenings to discuss what their school could become. While one might argue that what was needed here was more of a total faculty focus to open the lines of communication, there is much to be said for building toward such communication on the basis of subgroups (Schmuck, Runkel, Langmeyer, 1969). This group of teachers began an exciting series of meetings where the expected outcome was that of effecting changes in the teaching-learning environments in this school. Specifically, based on a kind of brain-storming approach as to how improvements could be brought about, four of the teachers decided to cluster their rooms together and to share grades one to five between them. Based on their enthusiasm and growing respect for each other's ideas and skills, they decided that under the existing environmental structure of one teacher with 30 children they were not being afforded opportunities to capitalize on their skills. Several felt badly that they were not able to use the strengths they had and were being asked to do things about which neither they nor the children were very excited. The implication is that they enjoyed different kinds of activities and if such enjoyment could be capitalized on by their helping each other, both they and the children would gain. The teacher's excitement generated by his enthusiasm for the subject could be contagious just as it is for many teachers when children become enthusiastic about a topic of their choosing. Under their proposed plan each teacher would spend time with the children in ways he felt most competent. One teacher would take the children for art, photography and crafts approaches; a second for math and science; a third for reading, remedial approaches and library skills with the school librarian assisting.

It is too early to ascertain whether what that group of teachers had planned was going to be effective. This underlying belief that perhaps by sharing time together teachers could get closer to the kinds of inner resources they had as human beings and as teachers and as a result assist in creating a climate for change in their public schools is an exciting one. One of the teachers involved in this sharing approach responded to the question of how they were doing by saying that she was just glad she and the others had "found" each other, that she had had no idea that they shared some of the same ideas and points of view. It seems almost revolutionary to teachers to tie together the harnessing of their skills and resources to effect changes in schools. There must be running rampant in the public schools either a high degree of pessimism as to how changes are brought about or an equally high feeling of mysticism that change may come but no one knows quite how. In the group of teachers that this book focuses on there developed a feeling that out of the combined strength each had acquired as a member of the group, they could make some translations to "back home" problems and situations. This issue of whether one is able to transplant what is gained in a group experience to the times that individuals function in ongoing organizational structures, such as schools, remains a large question. Nevertheless, teachers coming together in group process situations may, depending on the purposes for which such a group has been formed, be afforded an opportunity to get closer to who they are as people and what they would like to be with children.

It strikes us that in the public schools teachers are asked to and by necessity almost always focus on the realities of school, so much so that there is precious little time or energy for dreaming of what a school could be and what teachers could do in such schools that would allow them to maintain their integrity. For a number of reasons, generations of teachers seem to have been reared, or trained, on the premise that one's philosophy of teaching is a remote preoccupation bearing no relationship to their daily encounters with children. The group experience reported in this book, and several group approaches to be reviewed later, points toward the many daily applications of teaching philosophy that teachers can and do make in their work with children. In Lewin's terms, they have found that there is nothing quite so practical as a good theory, or at least a set of beliefs about the teaching-learning process.

SUMMARY

If we have learned anything it is that teachers are *real* human beings. They often find themselves expected to carry out society's mandate to "teach" their children while what it is that is to be taught remains blurred. The hurtful part of being a teacher seems to be the pressure to deny the kinds of feelings, needs, and concerns they harbor while going about the task of responding to children. In our work with teachers we have found relatively few who were not concerned with the children in their classrooms. To be sure, we did not always agree with their philosophy or feel kindly toward their style, but nevertheless, there should be room in schools for many types of teachers functioning according to their own styles, philosophies and consciences. And that is precisely what is not happening. Study of teachers and their classrooms will often reveal a power struggle of dramatic magnitude. It is adult against child. In the school at large there is an equally pervasive struggle for control. Is it the principal's school or does it belong to the teachers? What about the teachers' unions and their demands for safeguards? Now, of course, the power struggle has widened with the upsurge of interest in community control by parents. The tragedy behind this struggle is that no one really wants the schools. Teachers talk about "that" school and rarely internalize it as belonging to any part of their inner life; children's attitudes about school are mostly neutral (Jackson, 1968); and Greer (1969) points out that schools have never really met the needs of minority group children.

Our understanding of what teachers are asking is for the development of a partnership with others in the school and school community. In such a partnership the needs of the adults as well as the children would be considered. Our group of teachers clearly indicated that time in school cannot be solely *for* children. As adults they longed for meaningful contact with other adults. They were not just seeking approval for what they were doing, but they did want to share their ideas and hunches with others. They ran the constant risk of being rejected by other adults, thus being forced into a closer alliance with the children and finally, as a result, they experienced a loss of perspective from such constant and sustained contact with children.

REFERENCES

Beatles: Eleanor Rigby, P. McCartney & J. Lennon (BMI), 1966 (recorded music).

Gibbs, J. Is Help Helpful? *Forum* Association and Section Journal (YMCA) (February 1964), 25–27.

Greer, C. Public schools: Myth of the melting pot, *Saturday Review*, 1969, **52**, 84.

Jackson, P. W. *Life in classrooms* (New York: Holt, Rinehart & Winston, 1968).

Knoblock, P., Farrell, R., Lang, N., & Sullivan, A. A study of the characteristics of teachers of disturbed children and their preparation programs: An exploration of congruence as a criterion measure of effectiveness. Paper presented at the meeting of the Council for Exceptional Children, New York, March 1968.

Kohl, H. R. *The open classroom* (New York: New York Review of Books, 1969).

Schmuck, R. A., Runkel, P. J., & Langmeyer, D. Improving organizational problem solving in a school faculty. *Journal of Applied Behavioral Sciences*, 1969, **5**, 455–482.

II

Teachers in Groups:
The Search for Community

The previous section, describing loneliness, in terms of separateness and the breakdown in communications between adults, points to dilemmas of such large magnitude that active solutions are needed. It does not seem at all probable that the problems will go away on their own. Active interventions are needed mostly because of the destruction of the human spirit so poignantly reported by our group of teachers and by others.

Many purposes can be served by utilizing group process approaches. Just as there are many purposes which groups can aspire to, there are just as many varied group approaches. The following brief review of the literature addresses itself to the several ways in which group process experiences have been conceptualized and utilized with teachers. The descriptions which follow all lead to active involvement of teachers in the expression and solution of their concerns.

REVIEW OF GROUP APPROACHES UTILIZED IN
EFFECTING TEACHER CHANGE

After a rather extensive survey of the existing literature, we found relatively few reports of either a discussion or research nature which focused on teachers in groups. Most of what we uncovered had to do with teachers who were already employed and the group approaches utilized focused either on the obtaining of information, concepts, or perceptions or modifying their attitudes and/or behaviors through forms of mental health consultation. The last part of this section will highlight the rapidly developing sensitivity training movement with its focus on group process and development, and will attempt to relate concepts of such training to the functioning of teacher groups.

The major criterion for the inclusion of reports discussing group approaches with teachers is that of an interest in the growth of those participating. The purpose of the group, as indicated above, generated various definitions of growth, but it will be seen that even when the acquisition of concepts was at issue, individual and group growth was part of the focus. It is primarily the belief in the benefits of group process to foster such growth that has encouraged this book and our subsequent professional and personal efforts.

One of the earliest and most significant group interventions is that of Cantor's (1953) which involved a group of experienced teachers in a seminar. The seminar was an attempt to enable teachers to explore Cantor's notions of the following characteristics of skilled teaching:

1. The creation of an accepting atmosphere,
2. the structuring of a "reality-centered" classroom,
3. an awareness of the teacher's function and need to focus,
4. an understanding of when, how, and where to challenge the pupils,
5. an acceptance of the premise that learning is essentially personal, and
6. that it (learning) depends upon self-motivation and self-discipline. (p. 79)

In essence, the purpose of his group meetings was to engage the teachers in intensive discussion of the ingredients of the teaching-learning process, some of which included the above qualities of skilled teaching.

The style of leadership portrayed by Cantor has come to be known as "non-directive," but the label does not sufficiently convey what was done. In analyzing Cantor's statements, at least those chosen for inclusion in his book, it is clear that he served as a catalyst and clarifier. To be sure, he apparently harbored strong convictions as to what constituted teaching effectiveness, but one is impressed with his skill at getting the group members to critically evaluate their own stance on certain issues and feelings. One comes away from reading his book with a sense of excitement at having gotten closer to a teacher who honestly attempted to "practice what he preached." His behavior in the seminars closely paralleled his beliefs regarding what constituted skilled teaching. His procedures sought to create the kind of learning environment within the seminar which represented the very same issues which concerned teachers and children in classrooms. His basis for effective functioning of the teacher lies clearly within the interaction and relationship between the teacher and child. It was Cantor's goal that within this group process, the teachers could personally experience the characteristics of skilled teaching and thereby more fully experience themselves. Cantor, acknowledging that changes within the group members which could reasonably be expected to take place after one semester were limited, indicated that they did gain at least an intellectual awareness of the problems of teaching and learning. The practical carry-over of such learning into their work remained indeterminate.

Buckley (1954) conducted a 15 week group therapy series with teachers and specified his objective as improving their on-the-job functioning. Unlike Cantor's approach, this group approach did not begin from any theoretical position, but rather, "The objective of the group discussions was to create a social situation in which it would be socially acceptable to express positive and negative feelings and thoughts more freely and continuously" (p. 215). Buckley characterized this as analytic group discussion with the following set of ground rules:

1. Content is circumscribed and guided;
2. leader is permissive, accepting;
3. all members have a common background;
4. all members have agreed common objectives;
5. all members have joined out of their own free choice and desire. (p. 215)

From the brief descriptions of both Cantor's and Buckley's group approaches one can trace the development of much of the group literature with teachers which has appeared beginning in the 1950's. It will be of considerable assistance to the reader in understanding the dynamics of our group to look at the leader's behavior as reported in the various group studies and projects. Except in those group situations described as following a psychoanalytic-interpretive model, most leaders of teacher groups appear to see their role as that of enabler and catalyst for the group. Few of the projects have included a mixed group of school personnel, a strategy offering much potential. Certainly, our group experience dramatically highlighted the spill-over of feelings and relationship dilemmas to those other than children and fellow teachers. The inclusion of school administrators, classroom support personnel and possibly others might allow for more direct confrontations in exploration of the interpersonal miscommunications which seemed so evident, at least in our group experience. Following Buckley's listing of ingredients of analytic group discussion, the observation that all members have agreed upon objectives would not seem to be true in all of the reports surveyed. Or, if existing, such objectives were acted out and upon in a multitude of ways. Finally, it would be important to study the processes operating within such groups to gain a clear awareness of many of the above dimensions. In the majority of studies, including Cantor's and Buckley's, insufficient information is presented pertaining to phase sequence, the stages or phases through which the group progressed. Buckley maintains his objective was to assess and measure the outcomes rather than the process of the analytic group method. Our position is that it is quite impossible to fully assess and interpret one's outcome measures without clear specifications of the group process.

In a pilot project closely related to Buckley's (1954) interest in improving the in-school functioning of teachers, Nass (1959) utilized a group of graduate education students "to meet with a clinician to discuss such problems of adjustment as they might experience in the school situation." (p. 562) He refers to his approach as a psychotherapeutically oriented group, again confounding a clear understanding of what transpired by the use of still another group process label and not providing sufficient process and group dynamics information. Leader behavior is again described as that of a catalyst and "one of identifying underlying attitudes of the participants and using them as a basis for discussion." (p. 564) Nass described four discussion areas which he felt represented the difficulties facing new teachers: teachers' relationships with authority, their expectations of themselves as teachers, their relationships with colleagues, and their relationships with children. As will be seen in Parts III and IV dealing with teacher-pupil relationships, all of the discussion areas identified by Nass were of major importance to our group members also.

A series of reports (Berman, 1953, 1954; Snyder & Berman, 1960) offer us some comparison of group leader behaviors as well as of group process. In Berman's earliest report (1953) he utilized a combined seminar and psychoanalytic group method with guidance counselors, teachers and school administrators—one of the first published accounts to encompass such a diverse population. Part of his focus involved the presentation of didactic material followed by direct leader intervention as a group therapist. One of his tasks was to assist the participants in removing any "learning blocks" to the understanding and internalization of content material. Of interest for our purposes is his inclusion of selected analyses of phase movement, although not presented in a systematic manner nor using descriptive dimensions to aid in the analysis. Also, he describes throughout this series of articles, more direct involvement of the group leader who engaged in a good deal of interpretation of group behavior and feelings and seemingly controlled the flow of the group's life.

The representation of what transpired within group meetings was further elaborated upon in a report of a psychoanalytic group approach with teachers in a junior high school. (Snyder & Berman, 1960) A more extensive, but still selected summary of group sessions was presented. Again, one might decipher the phase movement but the task could have been made considerably easier by including more operational dimensions for the readers to focus upon. What appeared to be missing from this and the above studies utilizing a psychoanalytic model was a clear statement of objectives for the group in terms of movement.

In an interesting approach to forming a group of teachers, Daniels and his co-workers (Daniels, Snyder, Wool & Berman, 1960) reported how they began by organizing a group of predelinquent junior high school boys. Apparently interest and pressure were exerted by the teachers of these students to be given "equal time" and a similar group was formed for them. Gains and changes are again presented in discursive terms which makes precise analysis of what transpired difficult to understand.

This review of studies utilizing group process approaches with teachers has attempted to depict various ways such approaches can be designed. Keeping in mind that the purpose in virtually every study was to facilitate the growth of the participants, it is clear that the specific process and procedures may vary depending on a host of factors ranging from the style of leadership to the theoretical bias of the leaders or participants.

It is probably apparent to those readers who have had experience in schools that it is no small matter to bring a group of teachers together during the course of a school day. There are time pressures which have proven restrictive for many teachers but even more restrictive have been the lack of clear or relevant objectives behind involving teachers in a group process situation. The following sections discuss the usefulness of group approaches in meeting specific purposes and goals of the participants.

GROUP APPROACHES AS DATA COLLECTION

As indicated earlier, this project was begun as an attempt to gather the perceptions of teachers as to what their interactions with children looked like. To be sure, that purpose was accomplished, but it became clear that this was information gathering of a dynamic nature. For example, a teacher's relationships with children in the classroom are directly effected by and related to relationships with other adults. We experienced a feeling of sadness upon realizing how some teachers may be pulled toward the children because they, the children, are the only human contact afforded them in some schools. Depending on a teacher's gratification pattern and the kinds of needs being met outside of school, this may or may not be sufficient. It seems apparent that for many of the teachers who have talked with us there was a high degree of job satisfaction in school when their outside, and inside, experiences were adequate. While this seems like an obvious observation for many of us regardless of our job, it seems quite ignored when applied to teachers.

Nevertheless, as an approach or process for gathering information, group orientations have much merit. The dynamics of different individuals in the group fueling what another teacher has said provided us with considerable insight into the relationship dilemmas faced by them. Behaviors of group members often supported what another member was saying or served the purpose of asking questions of others that were really concerns of their own. We became particularly attuned to the use of questions by group members as a form of asking for information or the use of questions to really make statements. It often seemed that such questions were more often statements of their own concerns and the teachers were encouraged to state their feelings and observations directly. It seemed like magic to some group members when they realized others were voicing similar concerns. They asked for such validation of their concerns and in the process of asking more and more was uncovered both by the initiator of the discussion and from those responding to this person regarding their own inner feelings and reactions.

GROUP APPROACHES TO ENHANCE USE OF SELF

We have long felt that many teachers of difficult children, and perhaps other teachers as well, suffered under very pessimistic belief systems that prevented them from seeing themselves as potent forces in the lives of school children. Despite the popularity of the "Goodbye Mr. Chips" phenomenon or ideal, few teachers really believe they will be accorded that place in the hearts and memories of their classes. The sheer intensity of the day after day experience by definition almost prohibits a teacher from stepping back and seeing himself as a significant other to children.

One teacher in an urban school experienced extreme difficulty in providing a safe enough environment for her children. At Christmas she resigned, feeling that she was only a role for the children, that they didn't see her as a person and therefore there was no particular need for her to inform them that she wouldn't be back or any of the other changes that would take place upon their return. She softened her position somewhat and told them she wouldn't be returning. During the school vacation several of the children she had experienced the most difficulty with visited her at home. She was more than slightly surprised and quite gratified and proud that she had that kind of attraction or "pull."

The paradox is that parents probably receive more feedback from children regarding teachers than the teachers receive, and most of us hear parents complaining they don't hear enough about school from their children! The implication may be that if we believe teachers need feedback in order to use themselves as the vehicles of change in the classroom we may need to do as much with children to develop the kind of learning environment which will encourage and facilitate their offering feedback to teachers. The giving of feedback is only part of the issue; for teachers it is hearing the message and doing something with it!

We strongly believe that the teacher as person is the major resource for effecting change within the classroom. Admittedly this may seem to be a burden for some teachers since the responsibility seems a grave one. On the other hand, the recent outpouring of methods and materials has not seemed to appreciably enhance the learning and involvement of children and of teachers. It is interesting to note that George Dennison (1969) concludes his sensitive description of teachers and children with a statement of curriculum materials various teachers utilized. In almost every instance they were standard—that is material available to anyone; and perhaps most important of all, material that seemed to fit the particular goals and style of the teacher and children. One other observation could be made and that is in virtually every instance the material utilized was of an open-ended variety, that is to be manipulated and encountered by learners who could do things to and with the material. It was of an exploratory nature and children were not worked on by the material but they did the acting and reacting on it.

This discussion of materials is by way of saying that we are still left with the teacher as the resource for effecting change and not the material, curriculum, syllabus or what have you. In our group, however, this proved to be a difficult realization. In part, it had something to do with their prior experiences of frustration with children; but of even greater concern was their inability to see themselves as powerful or effecting others. In our group experience many members came to feel in closer touch with themselves in terms of their assets, liabilities and the kinds of aspirations they had for themselves. Our premise here was that with such increasing self-awareness there would tend to be fewer global self-judgments made by individual teachers about what they can and can't do. Along with an increase in self-awareness there also tended to be more accurate self-appraisals—that is, individuals came to see themselves as others saw them. We think this is terribly important in the life and school functioning of teachers. In the first place many teachers see themselves as invisible; they simply are *not seen* by others—adults or children. In our group such a distortion was diminished for many of the participants. They could come to see themselves as having something to say and do for others in the group. Our finding of a relationship between self perceptions and perceptions of others indicates in some ways the clarity of the person being viewed. And this is precisely what many teachers find so difficult to believe— that they have some kind of integrity and visibility as a person and that others see them that way. This group experience provided teachers with the opportunit to engage in self exploration and the other group members communicated that this was positively viewed by them and to be encouraged.

Our further premise is that the behavior of teachers in a group experience has great relevancy for how they could (and do) behave with children in their classrooms. We have some evidence for this in terms of the positive relationship between how group members and children rated individual teachers around interpersonal skills. This offered us some encouragement for viewing group process experiences as one way of effecting not only in-group behaviors but also classroom behaviors of the participating teachers.

GROUP PROCESS AS TRAINING IN GROUP SKILLS

The harsh reality of classroom life for teachers is that they are typically confronted on the first day of school with a group of children. If they have been taught any survival skills at all it is to "search" for the ring leader and neutralize his destructive influence. As a rule, however, training in the constructive utilization of group members is rarely a subject matter concern in preservice or inservice training experiences. In one urban school the principal arranged for his staff and teachers from others schools to enroll in a workshop focusing on the dynamics of groups. The following outline highlights the topics covered. It should be noted that within the context of substantive items there are built-in process approaches to the understanding of the content. For example, the use of role playing allowed some of those participating to try out new group role behaviors and others to attempt to respond accurately to such behaviors.

Inservice Experience
Staff Group Process Training[1]

1. To develop skills in listening to others.
2. To develop the skill to recognize and differentiate relevant and irrelevant areas of discussion.
3. To develop supportive skills (asking for and receiving feedback).
4. To develop source credibility (trust).
5. To develop self-analytical skills in identifying problems.
6. To develop group skills in solving mutual problems.
7. To develop group norms for helpful working relationships.
8. To develop the skill to deal productively with emotional responses.

It is our belief that the experiential dimensions of group process approaches allows for the acquisition of skills in responding to groups of children in a more meaningful manner than does a more didactic approach. Further, we would hold that teachers who are able to experience and try out new forms of group behavior will be in a better position to translate what they are personally learning into an interpersonal or interactional scheme. What we quickly realized was that part of the quandary for our group of teachers was that at the very same time that they were attempting to come to grips with their own life style they were being pressured and bombarded by other adults to

---

[1] This outline developed by W. Weber, Ph.D., School of Education, Syracuse University.

behave in rather different ways. We felt that in our group experience the participating teachers had an opportunity to see themselves, see others behaving, and view their behavior with others.

Certainly, in our efforts to increase the sensitivity and awareness of teachers there remains the lingering concern of whether they can incorporate sensitivity and awareness into their repertoire of skills for responding to children. This is analogous to the concern expressed in the preparation of therapists when it is realized that along with having an empathic understanding of the other person it is equally necessary to be able *to communicate* such understanding to the other person. Gage (1958), in a series of studies, investigated the relationship between the accuracy of teachers' perceptions of their pupils and their effectiveness as reported by the pupils. Most of his results did not show such a relationship. He offers several interpretations of the findings and one of ours would be that "understanding is not enough." The question then becomes how and in what manner does one acquire such skills.

Schmuck (1968) attempted to answer this very important question of how to design learning experiences for teachers which would enhance their functioning with classroom groups. He designed three projects which varied the experiential, didactic, and outside consultant experiences. Schmuck's findings lend strong support to an action-oriented approach to the acquisition of group skills for teachers. He found, as we did, that the discussions of what was and could happen in classrooms did much to increase a teacher's feelings of self worth, but the closer a teacher was able to get to actually trying new skills the more meaningful the new learning became. It became clear to us that there is a strong relationship between a teacher feeling good about himself and the utilization of new skills. In our group of teachers there were increased expressions by individual teachers that, as they came to see their own behavior more clearly, they were better able to sort out what was happening in their classrooms. To us one of the gratifying messages was that some began to see their relationship goal with children in classrooms as that of developing a partnership for learning. It seemed more possible with increased self-awareness to include the learner in the teaching-learning transaction.

The inservice proposal included above contained many group skills which appear important whether one is with a group of teachers or with a group of children. In many ways group sessions such as ours or the inservice proposal reported here serve as a testing ground for the acquiring and possible implementation of some of those skills in responding to groups of children. Again, Schmuck (1968) found that one of his groups which focused on effecting organizational change in the school was also able to translate some of what they learned from that focus into their classrooms.

SKILL ACQUISITION

Our group of teachers moved toward the developing of skills in listening and participating. The movement in this direction was slow and really only began to occur as relationships formed and the group members began to acknowledge that others had something to say and were representing themselves as open and real. Excerpts from our group sessions in Part III indicate the difficulty some group members had initially in listening and responding accurately to others. It proved to be difficult to confront individual members with observations as to how they were not attending to what was happening, but less difficult to express and accept when such *feedback* is based on the foundation of developing relationships in the group. Individuals would reflect on how and when they responded to children in their classrooms and the forms such feedback took. They reported that their responses to the child would frequently be based on where he as the teacher was and not often "listening" for the child's message.

In our group, and in other student and teacher groups, the asking for and receiving of feedback was a slow and agonizing process. Part of the frustration expressed by our group had to do with their uncertainty as to what to ask for and how to get it. In public schools many teachers will tell you that when they ask they often get more than they bargained for. In time, it became apparent to our group members that as individuals and members of a group they could offer support to other members. The reluctance and difficulty teachers have in seeing themselves as helpers of other adults remains a major paradox in schools. The development of skills that would enable group members to serve as resources for other teachers has great applicability to teaching in public schools. It has been our experience that in urban schools or in any school with difficult children a teacher who is having difficulty functioning receives "help" from everyone but other teachers. And more often than not, if the teacher is not able to summon up enough of his own inner strengths and skills, then he goes under. A few teachers we have known tried to and successfully assisted other teachers. In their reporting of such activities, however, they stated they didn't quite know how to go about it and "all they did was relate their own experiences." It seems to us that the development of supportive skills in teachers would provide many teachers with the awareness they need to be of help.

It became more apparent to our group members that how we spent our time forming our group, making decisions, solving problems, and developing group norms had relevance for the ways in which they as teachers spent time with children in classroom groups. Nowhere is it more dramatically obvious as to how inept teachers are at understanding group processes and acting upon their group skills than at many school faculty meetings where teachers serve as moderators. At such meetings, at least at the ones we have observed, the business is handled with dispatch, participation is limited to relatively few teachers who dominate, and dissatisfaction with what is happening is rampant, but never surfaces in explicit ways.

With our group of teachers their initial concerns about group behavior had more to do with their concerns about other staff members not wanting them at meetings and their own difficulty in remaining appropriately aggressive. Their time with groups of adults in schools often became nightmarish. At many such gatherings they often seemed to be taking an opposing point of view. This appeared to be translated by other teachers as siding and identifying with the children. What then typically happened was that as our group members became angry over what was being done to children and became more vociferous in objections they were more often tuned out and looked upon as deviant members of the group. They had then come full cycle: Not only were they teaching troubled children but they themselves had in fact become the deviant and difficult participants in their own peer group.

We believe that skills in responding to groups is best acquired by involvement in group process, particularly when the acquisition of group skills is made a conscious focus.

THE DEVELOPMENT OF TRUST

We found that participation and openness to others increased on the part of our group members but only after a period of time in the group had elapsed which allowed a basis for trust to occur. Of interest to us were group member perceptions as to what prevented trust from developing in their schools with their colleagues. For example, one teacher told of a colleague in her building who entered her classroom for the first time well after the school year had begun and exclaimed, "You have your children doing spelling and arithmetic!" Stunned by such a response at first, the teacher patiently explained what she and the children had been doing all these months and how she, too, was committed to children learning basic skills. Later, she grew more angry when allowed to puzzle over the very large issue of just how others in the school were perceiving her functioning—that of a non-teacher.

The issue of whether a teacher is teaching his children or behaving like a therapist or allowing uncontrolled things to happen has long been an issue between regular elementary education staffs and educators of difficult children. Recently, our experience in an elementary school has pointed out that even within a group of teachers supposedly all labeled as "regular classroom teachers" there is a degree of suspicion and distrust that fosters an oppressive atmosphere. In one faculty meeting the staff took a vote on policies dealing with how adults should respond to children's behavior. Not all of the staff present agreed with the majority. There was an expression of concern that as adults we were superimposing our values and beliefs onto the children. Several at the meeting, recognizing this cleavage, stated that now that a vote had been taken *all* should adhere to the majority decision. All of us know that in great numbers of instances voting changes little in the way individuals may actually *behave*. This particular vote had to do with children's swearing in school. It was not at all clear what profanity meant to everyone present, although it seemed clear to some. Many left that faculty meeting harboring feelings of distrust over the motives of others and the practices used at the meeting. The group practices utilized served only to mask the kinds of interpersonal concerns many teachers were experiencing with other staff members. It became more apparent that when teachers are faced with specific tasks that require coming together as a group they could profit from group training that encompasses procedures for interpersonal competence.

GROUP TRAINING FOR INTERPERSONAL COMPETENCE

One could argue that the environment of schools reward and reinforce highly organized activities. There has developed, in our opinion, a self-deceptive, no-nonsense climate which directly states that teachers are busy people and the demands upon their time are exhorbitant. While both of these claims may be true, it is our feeling that much teacher time has been spent in non-productive ways. In sum, it would appear that many teachers are weary of being "taught." The directive, didactic, "This is where you are wrong and what you can do about it" has been pushed about as far as possible in terms of sacrificing individual initiative and self-exploration.

For the above reasons, and for many others, educators have recently turned with great interest to a group-centered process popularly referred to as laboratory training, with sensitivity training one such form laboratory training can take. The broad objectives of such training have been described as:

1. Self-insight.
2. Better understanding of other persons and awareness of one's impact on them.
3. Better understanding of group processes and increased skill in achieving group effectiveness.
4. Increased recognition of the characteristics of larger social systems.
5. Greater awareness of the dynamics of change. (National Training Laboratories, 1967)

Basic to this training process are the reciprocal dimensions of risk-taking and feedback. By engaging in a degree of self-exposure one is maximizing his chances for reaction from others and at least a degree of self-confrontation. Unfortunately, the culture of many schools does not represent an open environment. What goes on in individual classrooms is revered beyond reasonable bounds. The ingrained notion that one is the master of one's fate as long as activities are confined to the four walls of the classroom is self-deception at its zenith. The lack of social and relationship accountability has provided teachers with a false sense of security.

A belief has been built up in the public schools that one of the advantages of being a teacher is that you are allowed to "do your thing"; but in practice you do it very quietly! Many classroom teachers find very early in their experiences, at least with the adults in schools, that risk-taking is not a highly valued activity. As a matter of fact there are some concerned critics of the public schools who maintain that much of what is wrong in schools has been studiously avoided. There are countless numbers of school personnel who simply "know" that whatever it is they want to do would be cut down by "someone up there." Assistant superintendents of schools hold their meetings and decide the "big man" wouldn't approve of certain decisions, while at the same time building principals have learned to cut through the red tape and go directly to the "big man" who usually approves of their idea if it can be substantiated. Classroom teachers tread gingerly to avoid breaking certain rules only to discover there was no such rule. It is a continuing paradox that public schools are at one and the same time the tightest and loosest organizational structures we have devised. Part of the difficulty teachers have had in taking risks has to do with minimum or negative feedback received for their actions. Our group of teachers expressed more than once the urge to act out and test the system in an effort to be noticed, valued and responded to. Again, this sounds remarkably similar to what children do with their teachers in an effort to gain a response.

In many ways then the concepts, techniques and processes utilized in sensitivity training may have much relevance to those functioning in educational institutions, and such techniques are in fact of growing interest to educators. To date, however, only one research study has appeared in the literature which applies to classroom teachers. Bowers & Soar (1961) conducted a well-designed study utilizing a pre and post design with 54 teachers, 25 of whom attended three weeks of half-day laboratory training. Ultimately, of course, the goal will be to maximize the effectiveness of teachers (as well as children) by use of differential group approaches matching teachers and programs according to process and outcome variables. (Harvey, Hunt & Schroder, 1961)

Bowers and Soar point out the values of experiential learning, of which their project was one example, insofar as such experiences allow the ideals of teaching to be incorporated in the training process. Their study highlights many of the parallels between ideals of teaching and the rationale of laboratory training. Such parallels could include the following:

1. Learning by experience is crucial to the changing of beliefs and attitudes. In education of children and adults we have probably over-emphasized the transmission of information and content as a way of effecting attitudes.
2. Increased awareness of how one is behaving in the form of feedback should be a part of every learning and training procedure. As our lives and environment become increasingly complex each new situation needs to be approached on the basis of our heightened awareness as to the impact we are having on others. It has become

more difficult to develop skills that are clearly generalizable to each new situation. On the other hand, the seeking of feedback as to how we are behaving and how our behavior affects others allows us to build a repertoire of behavioral skills that increase our sensitivity to self and others.

3. The practicing of skills in "safe" environments. So many school situations teachers find themselves in are "played for keeps." Confrontations and pressures can build up so fast that there is little or no opportunity to try new skills or to effect organizational changes so that new behaviors could be practiced. In one school a teacher was experimenting with the development of an open classroom concept in which children's becoming self-directed was given primary value. As the school year progressed pressures from other teachers mounted in terms of philosophical and practical differences as to how teachers should behave. This particular teacher remained calm when approached by some individual teachers and was responsive to their questions and concerns. She possessed a great many interpersonal skills but was not teaching within a very safe school environment. There was no process or set of procedures for non-threatening communication to occur. She felt at a loss and came to believe that she would need to expend her remaining energy on her classroom and "forget" the others. To translate, she was saying she would survive this school year but it wasn't likely she would expose herself to such abuse from other adults again.

4. An understanding of the dynamics of groups and individuals. At several points in this chapter we have touched on discrepancies between what teachers know and how they behave. Laboratory or experiential learning opportunities can enhance one's chances for testing out and improving one's understandings and actual skills. How exciting it is to envision the potential good which could accrue from practicing group behaviors with other teachers and then making such a translation to groups of children. Presently, the opposite seems to occur—that teachers' group behavior with other adults in school closely parallels how they control group behavior in their classrooms.

The Bowers and Soar study is rich with implications for the training of teachers where the training goal is that of increasing interpersonal competency. Advocates of laboratory training have pointed out that such procedures facilitate one's potential and are not necessarily aimed at major personality reorganization. This study found that attitude and personality measures predictive of "good" teaching were also predictive of those who profited from the experimental training procedure. They go on to say:

the same personal traits predict "good" teaching, with or without the training, but the training increased the degree of difference between greater and lesser skill. The effect of the training was to help the teacher realize his potential—to maximize the translation of his potentiality into actuality. A "good" teacher is made a better teacher as a result of the training procedure. (p. 141)

A comment regarding the experimental design and training procedures may be of help in understanding the above findings. Regular classroom teachers volunteered to participate, with 29 assigned to the control group and 25 to the experimental group. The experimental treatment took the form of two training laboratories conducted during the summer of 1959. Fourteen participated in the first and 11 in the second with the philosophy of training closely resembling that of the National Training Laboratory. (Bradford, Gibb, Benne, 1964)

Basically, three activities were utilized: 1) theory sessions in which concepts were presented in lecture presentations; 2) skill practice which involved structured activities such as role playing and group discussions and which often combined theory and skill practice; 3) training group (T group) activities which resemble group centered processes of an unstructured nature. These were conducted for two hours each day for three weeks.

More recently, there has been a rush of interest in applying laboratory techniques to human relations concerns in education and in schools. The applicability of sensitivity training to teachers and schools has been looked at in some quarters with reservation. In a lively debate published in *Phi Delta Kappan,* Thomas (1968) and Paris (1968) present the pros and cons of the translation of this approach into schools. Thomas maintains, "As now practiced, sensitivity training is a good idea gone bad." (p. 459) While he affirms the goals of such training, he takes issue with the ability of sensitivity training to aid teachers in reaching these goals.

Paris counters by pointing out that there are many possible designs for sensitivity training depending upon the specific goals and interests of the participants.

> T-Groups represent only one element, albeit the major one, in what is properly called the laboratory method or approach to education. Most laboratory method programs include a variety of other components in addition to the T-Group. These might include theory sessions, which are usually some kind of information giving and sharing meeting with an additional effort often made to involve the "audience" more directly in the educational process. Films are sometimes shown to dramatize an important issue. To provide experiences

with social systems of varying sizes, there are sometimes laboratory program elements involving two, three, or more people and including laboratory situations where two or more groups are involved as a larger community developing and sharing a common learning experience. (p. 461)

This brief outline of the range of laboratory designs by Paris is further elaborated upon in a thoughtful article by Argyris (1967), in which he discussed present laboratory designs which embrace the kinds of objectives cited earlier (NTL, 1967) and newer developments falling within a more existential framework. It seems clear, then, that the range of possible group approaches within any one framework is extensive and what is needed is a conceptual and investigative effort to cut through the labeling confusion with clear statements of the goals, processes and outcomes of such group approaches.

Moustakas (1957) applied a form of small group process with teachers in an effort to aid them to explore their behavior and relationships with children. In a two-semester seminar in interpersonal relations Moustakas obtained verbatim recordings of the actual sessions as well as written comments after each session and at the end of the course from each participant. In place of specifying concrete leadership techniques, Moustakas focuses more on the leader possessing a humanistic philosophy of man. For example, he comments:

We cannot teach another person directly nor can we facilitate oral learning in the same sense of making it easier. We can make learning possible by providing information, the setting, atmosphere, materials, and resources; and by being present in the full sense, through listening, empathizing, supporting and encouraging." (p. 73)

Paralleling in some major respects the kind of group meetings we conducted, his group discussed teacher-pupil relationships with the goal in mind of allowing each teacher to share with the other members "her own involvement with a child, the nature of this personal relationship, the possible development of a positive approach to the child, and a resolution of existing problems" (p. 75). A number of themes, apparent in our sessions as well, were identified by Moustakas. These include relationships with children, relationships with other teachers, relationships with parents, parent-teacher irresponsibility, parent-teacher cooperation, self-reference of the group, fear and freedom, and several educational issues including grades, punishment and praise. Moustakas notes:

The following conclusions were reached: (1) In an atmosphere of freedom where teachers are valued, fully accepted, and respected, a group of teachers is its own best resource and can serve as the primary basis for emerging insights and the resolution of problems. (2) Their most significant concerns are the personal relationships with the children, parents, and other teachers, rather than a concern over academic tasks. (3) Given the opportunity, teachers are capable of deep exploration and the discovery of basic issues and underlying values as well as related principles and facts. They develop a growing respect and empathy in personal relations, a deeper understanding of the unique personality of the child, and a broadening appreciation of the human element in all learning situations. (4) Self-discovery and professional insight, when there is freedom to explore and grow, comes from the teacher's own vital and dynamic experience. (5) Free open discussion in a strengthening climate, provides an opportunity for emotional release which frequently eventuates in broadened knowledge, in discovery of new classroom approaches to the individual child and to the group, and in modification of teachers' attitudes toward children, parents, and other teachers, in the direction of seeing the other person as potentially positive and healthy even in the light of defeating threats and pressures." (p. 92)

THE USE OF GROUPS IN THE PREPARATION OF TEACHERS

How remarkably obvious it seems to us to incorporate group experience into the preparation and inservice training of teachers—obvious because of the amount of time a classroom teacher is confronted with groups of children. The startling observation is that many teachers, whether they are dealing with regular or special classroom groupings, are approaching individuals within the group and failing to utilize group management approaches. Some very interesting research highlighting the efficacy and facilitative importance of group management and the development of a classroom has recently appeared (Kounin, Frieson & Norton, 1966; Kounin & Obradovic, 1968), lending impetus to a direct focus on groups.

One can only speculate as to the reasons for an almost complete avoidance of teacher's use of group process and dynamics in their everyday functioning with children. Undoubtedly, many teachers and other school workers will take issue with this interpretation of the behavior of many classroom teachers. There is rather convincing evidence stemming from the investigations of teachers' classroom behavior (Amidon & Hough, 1967) that great numbers of classroom teachers behave in rather autocratic ways and neglect to bend to the group needs of their children. It is our rather strong belief that guided experience in understanding one's own group behavior and the management of groups is a necessary prerequisite to effective functioning with groups. While there are texts written on dynamics of classroom groups, without a personal frame of reference for group participation the application of sound techniques remains elusive. We were left with the distinct impression from our group project that for most of those participating it was the first "real group experience" they had experienced. While most of us, like children in schools, are exposed to many groups and many living situations revolving around group life, we somehow manage to maintain our individual identity on one level, but on another level function in spite of the group. To be part of, while at the same time to be apart from, the group is a common experience many of us share.

The preparation programs of teachers have tended to ignore the potential learning material to be found within their own institutions. We need to look no farther than a *program* for teachers of emotionally disturbed children or an elementary education preparation *program* to come up with a ready-made group to focus on as an *in vivo* experience. How real the curriculum of expanding one's awareness of groups could be made if the training group is encouraged to study their own group life together.

We are saying, then, that one of the outcomes of a teacher preparation program should be the utilization of all available experiences as training data, including the very experiences one is going through en route to the goal of becoming a "teacher." The goal would be, in the words of Forst and Matthews (1964) . . . "to apply the principle that what is taught is more likely to affect action if it is learned in relation to action." In their article, the objective was to teach the concept of democracy to teachers in training by exposing them to a group process experience which attempted to represent democratic procedures in its structure and functioning. The attempt was to coordinate and integrate the presenting of facts regarding education in a democracy but learn such content within a democratically organized learning environment.

The translation of the attempt by Forst and Matthews to other "content" and training areas is easily made. In those teacher preparation programs in which the student group is highly visible due to the specialized nature of their training it seems a logical and short step to have them focus on their own friendship patterns; the relationships between their in-class and coffee shop behavior with each other; the members of their program who do not participate and interact; how as a collective body they can generate strong feelings toward the faculty and courses while milder thoughts might be harbored as individuals.

The hypothesis is that the learning of group dynamics and the understanding of group processes can be made more personally meaningful, and that the transfer to one's professional behavior with children would be expedited and enhanced. As is the case with other areas of the literature surveyed to this point, there is a dearth of reported studies, but what has been done will be looked at in light of this hypothesis.

The Forst and Matthews report is a rather unique one in that much of what is presented is from the point of view of leader behavior. The specific steps and stages the leader went through are detailed as are the specific fluctuations in feelings that coincided with the particular topic or format for any given day. The reader is given the rare opportunity to sit in on the actual "lesson plans" designed by the group and leader and then evaluate the outcome as reflected in the leader's reactions. In their analysis of outcomes, complete reliance on student comments is presented as evidence, although the authors do acknowledge the validity problems inherent in presenting this as sole evidence. They indicate that three-fourths of the final evaluation comments were positive:

> The positive comments seem indicative of attitude shifts, which may be classified according to my teaching objectives as (1) gains in appreciation of democratic values, (2) development of social sensitivity and social skills, (3) increased autonomy in learning, and (4) change in attitude toward teaching and the teacher's role. (p. 412)

This approach involving the total immersion of trainees and the blurring or merging of content and process for learning is also represented by studies using education majors in role playing situations. For example, Johnson and Rau (1957) utilized sociodrama in a small teacher training college campus. Their premise was that entering college students are confronted with group relationships centering on student to administration, student to faculty, student to student, and student to community relationships. The authors note that: "If he makes a satisfactory adjustment to these basic groups, then he is likely to acquire that attitude of mind so requisite for the end result—the socially-conscious teacher." (p. 93)

It seems clear to us that if teachers are to be expected to respond to and relate with groups of children, then a logical way to facilitate such skills is in the preparation of teachers. If prospective teachers can experience group process approaches, skills, and techniques then we believe they can more realistically make an adequate translation to the realities of classroom and school group life.

WHAT IS IT THAT TEACHERS ARE ASKING? A SUMMARY STATEMENT

It is our belief that the utilization of group process approaches with teachers provides one training opportunity for gaining a sense of community with others. At the same time this approach supports the development of skills which can be utilized both with children in classrooms and with other groups of adults in school.

Argyris (1968) has pointed out how extremely difficult it is to gain interpersonal competence when one's survival needs are high. Our teachers' reports are ample evidence for the observation that their feelings of adequacy and performance with children were tied closely to their interactions with other adults. When lines of communication and opportunities for the development of satisfactory adult relationship were limited, then no matter how "successful" they might be with children they found teaching a desperately lonely experience.

This portion of the book has attempted to describe some of the values inherent in a group process approach as one alternative for diminishing teacher loneliness and concern. More and more teachers are recognizing various alternatives that they have or are setting about to create options for communicating with others. The following suggestions just begin to scratch the surface of possibilities that are either available or could be encouraged by active and involved teachers.

1. There is growing interest in teacher self-help experiences taking form in self-directed or leaderless groups in which those participating design the experience and are responsible for its implementation. Such self-directed groups could focus on a variety of teacher concerns including child management concerns, introduction of educational innovations into the school, and school issues such as community involvement and parent-teacher relations.
2. Teachers have the option of asking their administrators for a voice in decision-making as another way of taking an active part in seeking solutions to faculty school communication patterns.

3. There are now many groups and trained professional workers who could assist a school staff in designing a staff development process. In some school systems such trained persons are even employed by the system.
4. Teachers could help articulate a role for school psychologists which could include forms of mental health consultation for teachers focused on their children, their own personal or professional concerns or all of these.
5. There may be many informal efforts by teachers to involve other teachers in sharing and talking with each other. "Buddy" systems of teachers using team and grade level meetings to discuss feelings as well as facts is one approach.
6. Certainly much can and should be done with school faculty meetings in order that they present a model of how people could communicate and share with each other rather than an experience to be avoided or at best tolerated.
7. Many approaches could be used to involve oneself with other adults in the school. They could range from encouraging other adults to spend time in classrooms to asking for and giving feedback to others.
8. Teachers could take an active part in the designing of inservice experiences in order to guarantee the relevance of such experiences.

Parts III and IV will also highlight the internal concerns our teachers had about their behaviors with children. Invariably they found themselves unable to gain a perspective on how they behaved. The group process situation they experienced and which is reported in this book was one attempt to provide such a perspective.

REFERENCES

Amidon, E. J., & Hough, J. B. (Eds.) *Interaction analysis: Theory, research and application* (Reading, Mass.: Addison-Wesley, 1967).
Argyris, C. On the future of laboratory education, *Journal of Applied Behavioral Sciences*, 1967, **3**, 153–183.
_____ Conditions for competence acquisition, *Journal of Applied Behavioral Sciences*, 1968, **4**, 147–177.
Berman, L. The mental health of the educator, *Mental Hygiene*, 1954, **38**, 422–429.
_____ Mental hygiene for educators: Report on an experiment using a combined seminar and group psychotherapy approach, *Psychoanalytical Review*, 1953, **40**, 319–332.
Bowers, N. D., & Soar, R. S. Evaluation of laboratory human relations training for classroom teachers. Studies of human relations in the

teaching-learning process: V. Final Report. U. S. Office of Education, Contract 8143 (Columbia, S.C.: U. of South Carolina, 1961).

Bradford, L. P., Gibb, J. R., & Benne, K. D. (Eds.) *T-group theory and laboratory method: Innovation in re-education* (New York: Wiley, 1964).

Buckley, F. M. Use of the analytic group discussion method with teachers. In M. Krugman (Ed.), *Orthopsychiatry and the school* (New York: American Orthopsychiatric Association, 1954).

Cantor, N. *The teaching–learning process* (New York: Holt, Rinehart & Winston, 1953).

Daniels, E. M., Snyder, B. R., Woll, M., & Berman, L. A group approach to pre-delinquent boys, their teachers, and parents in a junior high school, *International Journal of Group Psychotherapy*, 1960, **10**, 346–352.

Dennison, G. *The lives of children* (New York: Random House, 1969).

Forst, F., & Matthews, J. Preparing teachers by exposure to group processes, *Journal of Teacher Education*, 1964, 404–414.

Gage, N. L. Explorations in teachers' perceptions of pupils, *Journal of Teacher Education*, 1958, **9**, 97–101.

Greer, C. Public schools: Myth of the melting pot, *Saturday Review*, 1969, **52**, 84.

Harvey, L. J., Hunt, D. E., & Schroder, H. M. *Conceptual systems and personality organization* (New York: Wiley, 1961).

Jackson, P. W. *Life in classrooms* (New York: Holt, Rinehart & Winston, 1968).

Johnson, M. R., & Rau, G. G. Sociodrama applied on a teacher training college campus, *Peabody Journal of Education*, 1957, **35**, 93–96.

Kounin, J. S., Frieson, W. V., & Norton, A. E. Managing emotionally disturbed children in regular classrooms, *Journal of Educational Psychology*, 1966, **57**, 1–13.

———— & Obradovic, S. Managing emotionally disturbed children in regular classrooms: A replication and extension, *Journal of Special Education*, 1968, **2**, 129–135.

Moustakas, C. Self-explorations of teachers in a seminar in interpersonal relations, *Journal of Individual Psychology*, 1957, **13**, 72–93.

Nass, M. L. Characteristics of a psychotherapeutically oriented group for beginning teachers, *Mental Hygiene*, 1959, 562–567.

National Training Laboratories. *Reading book: Twenty-first annual summer laboratories in human relations training* (Washington, D.C.: NTL Institute Applied Behavioral Science, 1967).

Paris, N. M. T-grouping: A helping movement. *Phi Delta Kappan*, 1968, 460–463.

Schmuck, R. A. Helping teachers improve classroom group processes. *Journal of Applied Behavioral Sciences,* 1968, 4, 401–435.

Snyder, B. R., & Berman, L. The use of a psychoanalytic group approach with teachers at a junior high school. *American Journal of Orthopsychiatry,* 1960, 30, 767–779.

Thomas, D. T-grouping: The white-collar hippie movement. *Phi Delta Kappan,* 1968, 458–460.

III

A Group Process with Teachers

We're alone together now,
—MARY, Group
SESSION NINE

INTRODUCTION

The group as an entity will be the focus of the present section. Major group forces and characteristics will be examined over the course of the group's life and, in doing so, we will seek by means of a session by session analysis to describe the group's halting movement toward change in its members, the ebb and flow of constructive and retarding events and, more generally, the group as a process. Included in this analysis will be focus upon such dimensions as the group's development of cohesive structure (and the complementary characteristics of resistance and loneliness), the group's phase movement in both content and quality of interaction across sessions, and the group's leadership patterns. Since so much of our subsequent examination of the group will emphasize these three dimensions—cohesiveness, phase movement and leadership—it seems instructive to begin this chapter with a brief consideration of the relevant bodies of research literature.

Cohesiveness

Early investigations of small group cohesiveness reveal three rather different definitions of this group characteristic: (1) the attraction of a group for its members, (2) members' motivation to participate in the group's activities, and (3) the coordination of the efforts of group members. The latter two definitions relate primarily to productivity and achievement motivation, whereas the first, as Golembiewski (1962) notes, involves a generalized group property and motivation for mem-

47

bership per se. Schachter, et al. (1960), as well as other investigators, have demonstrated that groups toward which members are highly attracted may develop norms resulting in low group productivity and low achievement motivation. Thus attraction, participation motivation and coordination were found to not necessarily go hand in hand. Small group researchers responded to such findings by narrowing the range of phenomena subsumed under the concept of cohesivness, with member attraction to the group becoming its major definitional focus. Cohesiveness thus defined became, and has remained, a popular variable for investigation—largely due to its considerable power in influencing many dimensions of small group behavior. Concretely, it has been demonstrated that members of highly cohesive groups, in contrast to groups in which intermember attraction is low, will:

1. Be more open to influence by other group members.
2. Be more accepting of member hostility.
3. Place greater value on the group's goals.
4. Experience greater anxiety reduction.
5. Participate more equally in group discussions.
6. Participate more actively in group discussions.
7. Exert more pressure on marginal group members.
8. Be less susceptible to disruption as a group when a member leaves the group.
9. Find greater agreement regarding the group's status hierarchy.
10. Remain in the group longer.
11. Be absent less often from group meetings.

Thus one may conclude that small group cohesiveness is a powerful variable indeed, one strongly influencing a wide array of cognitive, interpersonal and behavioral aspects of member functioning.

We will shortly turn to an examination of the development of intermember attraction in our teacher group, focusing on both its antecedents and consequents. At this point in our presentation, it is perhaps sufficient to note that most of the group's members were unknown to each other prior to the group's organization.

Phase Movement

We will be seeking in this part to describe and analyze the teacher group from a variety of perspectives, but one of our major emphases will be on the group as a fluid, changing entity. As an aid in bringing a modicum of order out of fluidity, an examination of the phases through which the group passed will be worthwhile. A number of investigators have focused upon phase sequences as they have emerged in groups of various kinds. Bales (1951), for example, in his investigation of problem solving groups reports the regular occurrence of three stages during the course of a group's functioning. The first, Orientation, is characterized largely by the offering and seeking of information and clarification by the group members. Evaluation, the second phase, consists primarily of the exchange of opinion, analysis and the expression of feeling. The final phase, Control, involves direct suggestions for problem resolution. While Bales and Strodtbeck (1951) report such phase movement for groups meeting for only one or a few sessions, it is worth noting that Psathas (1960) found similar orientation-evaluation-control movement across sessions of psychotherapy groups. Such regularities in group behavior, however, are influenced to varying degrees not only by the rating scheme used by the investigator, but also by the group's goals, its specific membership, the nature of its leadership, and the structuring provided group members. Martin & Hill (1957), for example, describe a phase sequence in psychotherapy groups—which is similar to, yet goes beyond that identified by Bales. The stages they identify are:

1. Individual unshared behavior in an imposed structure.
2. Reactivation of fixed interpersonal attitudes.
3. Exploration of interpersonal potential within the group.
4. Synthesizing interpersonal experience into group relevant orientations.
5. Consciousness of group dynamics and group process problems.
6. The group as an effective integrative social instrument.

Bach's (1954) description of communication phases in psychotherapy groups is even closer to what transpired in our teacher group, but even here some important differences between the two exist, e.g., phase 3 was minimal in our group and phase 5 was non-existent. Bach lists:

1. Stereotyped rational problem-solving.
2. Nonstereotyped, didactic-directive.
3. Cathartic verbalization and play.
4. Testing of interpersonal effects.
5. Contextual associates (free association).
6. Self-perception.
7. New problem solving.

The phase sequences reported for T-groups by Bradford, et al. (1964) and for problem solving groups by Golembiewski (1962) further illustrate the manner in which group goals, membership, leadership and structuring can all influence the flow of group functioning. It is important to underscore at this point that our teacher group was *not* conceived of as either a psychotherapy group, a T-group or as a problem solving group per se but, instead, as an admixture of all three. That is, our intent with this group was, like a therapy group, to increase member self-awareness; like a T-group, to increase their interpersonal sensitivity; and, like a problem solving group, to help them come to grips more effectively with teacher-pupil problem situations arising in their daily lives.

With this triad of goals in mind, we envisioned a three phase group development. In order to capitalize on the members' usual approach to pupil problem resolution, we planned to permit them to focus initially on specific, problem pupils while the group leaders began to wean them away from this exclusive pupil-is-the-problem orientation by consistently inquiring into the teacher's contribution to the given classroom conflict. We concretely operationalized this first phase by requesting the group members, in turn from sessions 3 through 8, to "present a case." During this first phase, as will be noted when we shortly turn to our session by session analysis, a beginning understanding emerged in the group regarding *their* contribution to classroom dynamics. To move further in this direction, beginning with session 9, we formally left the *Pupil Centered Phase* of the group and entered the *Teacher-Pupil Relationship Phase*. Here, each teacher was requested, in turn during sessions 9 through 14, to re-present his or her problem pupil but this time to do so with a singular emphasis upon the teacher and teacher-pupil relationship dimensions of the problem situation. The final phase, overlapping with the second but coming to fullest bloom during sessions 15 through 17, involved *New Problem Solving*. Here, self-insights gained in discussion of within-group relationships and relationships with specific pupils were generalized to other pupils, other school relationships and to other dimensions of self-awareness.

A content analysis to verify major aspects of this phase sequence was conducted. All statements made during sessions 2, 6, 10 and 14 were categorized in terms of their referent, i.e., Pupil, Self or Other Group Member. To the extent that our planned phasing was successful, Pupil statements should predominate during early sessions and then decrease; whereas Self referring statements and statements relevant to the behavior of Other Group Members should be infrequent at first and then increase substantially. As Table 1 indicates, this is precisely what transpired, thus attesting to the success of implementing the planned phase movement.

TABLE 1   Phase sequence of topics discussed

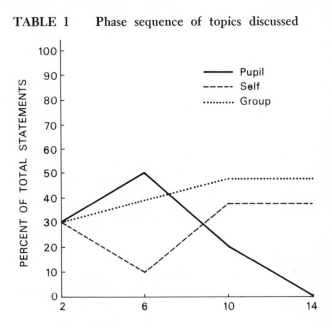

Leadership

Group Leader orientation may be described along a dimension whose poles are leader-centered and group-centered. In group psychotherapy, the leader-centered approach would be reflected by a therapist who tended to be directive, interpretive and who focused on the psychodynamics of individual group members. The group-centered psychotherapist is less overtly active, more of a catalyst or encourager of member-to-member and not member-to-therapist interaction, and more oriented toward groupwide influences on individual patients. Champions of both positions abound. Locke (1961), Lowrey (1944), Wolf and Schwartz (1962) and others favoring a psychoanalytic stance lean toward leader-centeredness, or what they have termed "therapy *in* a group." Contrastingly, "therapy *through* a group" has been more closely associated with a non-directive group psychotherapy position, e.g., Bion

(1959) and Hobbs (1951). While a similar split in preferred leadership orientation is evident in the small group literature dealing with non-psychotherapy groups, an overall tendency toward group centeredness is apparent. Research reports have increasingly yielded support for the efficacy of such group centeredness. Gordon (1955), focusing upon classroom leadership, has noted:

> In summarizing the results of these eleven studies of leadership, all carried out in educational settings, it can be stated with a high degree of confidence that group-centered leadership in the classroom situation is not only possible but also beneficial in many respects. Students seem to learn as much or more factual information; they participate more; they enjoy the experiences, and they acquire certain other important learnings, such as clinical insight, greater personal adjustment, socially interpretive behavior, skills of working cooperatively with others, and the freedom to communicate their deeper feelings and attitudes. Finally, when these student groups are given certain tasks requiring group judgment or group decisions, those with group-centered leadership demonstrate more effectiveness in altering individual judgments in the direction of a group norm, than do groups with directive or leader-centered leadership. (pp. 99-100)

While less unequivocal, the group psychotherapy research literature points in related directions. Goldstein, Heller, and Sechrest (1966), after examining several investigations of group therapist behaviors, conclude that the most effective orientation seems best characterized as "modified group-centered," that is, an essentially group-oriented approach that makes selective, carefully considered use of therapist interventions and involves therapist activity under selected circumstances, but activity used in such a manner that the basic group-centered orientation is not disturbed.

Three persons were involved, directly or indirectly, in the leadership of our teacher group—the two group leaders who actually conducted the meetings and a consultant with whom the leaders met weekly for a discussion of the preceding meeting, the group's progress and problems, and the planning of future strategy. Both the consultant and one of the group leaders, in response to the research literature we have just considered, sought to have the group led in accord with principles of modified group-centeredness. This group leader, Jack, was consistently successful in this regard and thus most frequently enacted his leadership role by serving as a facilitator and group catalyst. Will, the other group leader, differed from Jack in professional training and orientation to group leadership. Consistent with his orientation, he behaved throughout the course of the group's meetings in a highly active, directive, and at times forceful manner. In a didactic sense, these contrasting approaches to group leadership will be most worthwhile examining in our session by session analysis because their reflected consequents in the behavior of group members proved to be markedly different from one another.

Session 1.   Where Are We?

The purposes of the group were structured to each member when the initial invitation to join was extended. Structuring, however, is necessarily a continuing process and, further, a process best achieved by members actually experiencing the group in action. Most of this first session, therefore, were attempts by the members to obtain experiential information regarding the group's ground rules. While in both the initial structuring and in their comments during this first session, the group leaders urged a focus upon *both* pupils and the teachers themselves, certain forces served to make this session very strongly pupil-centered. We speak here of initial resistance and disclosure anxiety, phenomena observed in many types of groups whose goals require personal disclosure. Thus, consistent with our plans for phase movement and development, little *direct* progress was made during this session toward teacher-centeredness or toward focus upon the teacher-pupil relationship. It is clear, however, that groups such as these must first pass over certain intermediate hurdles before a measure of genuine openness and trust can be reached. One of these hurdles is group cohesiveness and, on this dimension, it is quite clear that the group achieved satisfactory initial progress.

The behavior of certain individuals during this session was noteworthy not only as it served to shape the session itself, but also as predictive evidence for behaviors which emerged more fully as later sessions unfolded. Ken, for example, was clearly the most actively resistive group member during this first session. He forced the exclusive pupil focus, interdicted leader attempts to wean the group away from this focus and, in doing so, offered the group a barrage of intellectualized, distancing and "safe" observations regarding pupil management. All of this he continued to do far into the group's life, well after all other members had ceased to do so. Similarly predictive was the behavior of Jack and Will, the group leaders, during this first session. Jack was feeling-oriented and, in a consistent manner, sought to make it comfortable for group members to focus upon *their* contribution to teacher-pupil interactions. Will was information-oriented and, in most aspects of his group interactions, behaved as another group member. Jack seemed to be viewing the group largely as a sensitivity group; Will operated as if it were a discussion group. In very large measure, these discrepant leader behaviors continued throughout all group sessions.

With regard to the actual content of this session, as was implied above, techniques for managing problematic pupil behavior were the major substantive theme. It is noteworthy, however, that even in this first session—with disclosure anxiety maximal and cohesiveness minimal —the theme of teacher loneliness emerged, as it was to do in one guise or another during almost every group session.

In an abstract and largely depersonalized manner, the first several minutes of this session were spent in sharing philosophies of managing problem pupils. It was "getting acquainted time" with all group members behaving in a friendly and agreeable—if superficial—manner. Jack and Will were rather silent and Ken was the most talkative member. Past and current teacher experiences were shared in a context of apparently tension-reducing good humor. It was in some ways a testing-out time, a time to tentatively assess one's group mates. The group's joking during this opening segment about humor in their classroom appears to provide our first example of the ways in which events outside the group are discussed as a means of helping the discussants define within-group boundaries. Ken, for example, the member most anxious at this point in time, commented:

> I'm getting a lot of humor that would come out in a classroom, a normal classroom. But they do it to see what I am going to do. I don't think I could do the same thing to them because they don't buy jokes. They really don't think you're kidding and it's difficult to joke with them.

We view this comment as likely representing Ken's concern about how he and his humor were coming across in the group, i.e., "are the other teachers buying me" he seemed to be asking.

Also quite early in this session, the group leaders teamed up in their first attempt to shift focus toward the teachers themselves. The group's high level of resistance as well as the subtlety of the attempt itself caused it to succeed only very briefly. As noted in the sequence below, the group then quite rapidly returned to their exclusive pupil focus.

Jack: You're saying when youngsters act out humorously they are
          exposing more of themselves. Is that what you're saying?
Helen: Yes.

Jack:	I can't help but think of when adults tell jokes to one another. How often people will not admit that they don't understand it.
Will:	Or how long does it take before you will perhaps tell a joke in a group?
Betty:	I'll explain it later, please laugh now.
Barbara:	And how you laugh in a group at the not funny jokes just to be a member of the group.
Mary:	So what are we suggesting we do? Teach an appropriate emotion?
Ken:	I don't know. I wonder what happens to the teaching. It's hard to teach a joke.

The group continued its exclusive pupil focus and, about a third of the way through the session, Jack responded with more direct cueing toward the topic of the teacher's involvement. But this too proved to be too early in the group's life to elicit the response sought.

Jack:	Maybe we have to go back another step. I thought this is what you were getting at before. Just from the tone of the conversation we've had here and the kind of affect that is coming out and the loud laughter about relating some of the incidents, can we talk about teaching the youngster and forget about the teacher who is doing the teaching? From what you folks have been saying, it seems like this is a pretty emotionally charged topic.
Barbara:	There was something else. He comes back and he says Walt Disney died, but he'll come back to life, won't he? Once we work through this, everybody dying, they've got to come back to life. My uncle died, he's going to come back to life.
Helen:	Is this an uncle he wished to death, or had the uncle died?

At this point in the sequence, Will forcefully supported Jack's attempt to arouse a teacher-focus, and Barbara just as forcefully reaffirmed her unreadiness to do so.

Will:	What is he trying to do to *you*?
Barbara:	Well, he does this to everybody.
Will:	And he's doing it to you too. Let's forget everybody else. I'm sure you're like everybody else in some ways, and in other ways you're selective, but what is he trying to do to you?
Barbara:	As I say, a part of it is when he makes somebody die, he's angry at you. And this is his best weapon against you.
Will:	So how is he trying to make you feel?

Perhaps of greatest consequence with regard to the foregoing exchange is the issue of timing. Group members will not, in almost any group, reveal their private feelings until they have experienced the group sufficiently to feel relatively safe, i.e., that the potential rewards of disclosure outweigh the rewards of guardedness. At this point in the group's life, guardedness was preferred and was perhaps even augmented by Will's directive approach. Just how strong such resistance can be, how far from oneself one can place the group's interaction, is well illustrated by a statement made by Ken shortly after the above excerpt:

> Now, as a teacher in reaction to that, don't you have to conclude why he's doing this? I can name about three or four reasons why a child might use that particular response. He can fear death, really and you'd move in on that in a certain way. He might have an inappropriate behavior . . . he has the right emotion, but he doesn't know how to express it. It's a good way to control people. You have to conclude why he's using it, and then move in a certain way.

We view this statement, whose diagnostic accuracy is largely irrelevant to the group's purpose, as Ken's attempt to provide himself with a safe and seemingly sage screen behind which to hide. As noted earlier, this type of verbalization was repeated by Ken well into the group's life.

The group members persisted throughout the remainder of this session in focusing upon the "how to" of pupil management, while the leaders encouraged a "feel about" perspective. Although the members were only minimally responsive to this urging toward openness in any direct sense, much did transpire during this session to augur well for openness at later sessions. A marked universalization effect occurred, i.e., a frequent, group-wide sharing of common problems. Cohesiveness was clearly elevated over its pre-session level. And, we can assume, a good bit of implicit structuring toward teacher-centeredness was successfully delivered by the group leaders.

Perhaps much of what this first session did accomplish from the perspective of the members is captured in a closing statement relevant to both cohesiveness and loneliness made, significantly, by Ken:

> Things happen in a classroom. You feel a certain way and it's awful nice to know someone else does. There is not that much opportunity to validate it within the school system because all the other classes are different and when you talk to someone all the other viewpoints are different and twenty to one you start to worry.

Session 2.   Enter Loneliness

All major themes of the initial session continued during the second group meeting. The content focus was again fairly exclusively upon the group members' pupils. The group leaders continued the structuring process. There was much "rallying around" by the teachers in the group, particularly in making common cause in hostility toward the "regular" teachers in their respective schools. The leaders, and Jack in particular, continued seeking to make it comfortable for the members to focus upon their contribution to teacher-pupil problem interactions. Communication among the members was widely dispersed. Cohesiveness continued to grow, although it is important to note that during this early stage of the group's development the bases for this growing level of intermember attraction were occupational similarity (special education teacher) and shared alienation (from "regular" teachers) and not the more fundamental and enduring basis of relatively full and accurate knowledge of one another—as was to develop several sessions hence.

In the opening moments of this session, Barbara made use of a number of technical, psychological terms in presenting her impressions of a specific pupil. This use of "psychological language," coming as it did from most group members at various points during the course of the group meetings, is of dual interest in that it both caused and reflected a basis for both their alienation from other teachers in their schools and their attraction to one another in the group. Stated otherwise, one might suggest that common language makes for camaraderie while language divergencies augment alienation.

Bach (1954), writing with reference to psychotherapy groups, notes the frequent occurrence of what he terms "set-up operations," which he defines as an unconscious attempt by a group member to elicit behaviors from the other members which will satisfy his (the originator's) needs. This is precisely what Barbara appears to have engaged in at the beginning of this session, seeking in a plea for universalization, to elicit sympathy and support from her fellow group members. As the excerpts below illustrate, the set-up attempt not only worked, it worked too well. Barbara apparently became aware of the personalized implications of the course of group discussion, felt uncomfortably "center stage" and successfully sought to get the group's spotlight directed back to pupil concerns.

Barbara: You know one thing that's been bugging me this week, and I wanted to get some others' opinion on it, because I wonder if it's going on in other places or other people have this same question or the same troubles . . . of how to get other people to see the group contagion that goes on with emotionally disturbed. A lot of people see them on an individual basis, or they see them walking through the hall and a lot of them say, gee, that kid is pretty good. You keep trying to tell them, you know, you should see him in the group. Everybody I think thinks you're rationalizing or something and I just wondered if anybody else had the problem because it's bugging me.

Mary: Therefore, to them he's really not disturbed, he doesn't seem to be when they see him. Is that what you mean?

Barbara: They are seeing him a lot more healthy.

Mary: Not what they expect a disturbed child to be.

Barbara: Right.

Will: That's what I mean, you're the bearer of the bad news.

Barbara: Right, I'm the problem.

Ken: Can't they observe your class?

Barbara: No.

Ken: Could they?

Barbara: Well, they . . . they see him (pause). Well, I didn't want to get this personally. I didn't really mean to bring it down to my individual basis. I just wondered if others had this.

Pat: I think I have it in all possible ways.

Helen: What we're getting into is the lack of understanding of what this type of child is.

Implicit in the content of this excerpt is the notion of alienation from or loneliness with regard to regular teachers, i.e., the school peers of the group members. The group members rallied around this topic and in an active, group-wide discussion early in this session they began to identify further sources of aloneness for them within the school culture. Helen, for example, commented:

You work with the kids with kid gloves. I mean all my energies are the kids. I get frustrated when I have to put the same kid gloves on and brownie and do all those things with adults, to appease feelings and everything else. Like today I called for a crisis person and she wasn't able. It was a severe crisis and one of the student social workers came down, and I said I'm sorry I can't use you, would you please get . . . oh, she was so offended, she talked to the social worker, she brought it up at the meeting, and said she felt unwanted. I said you were unwanted in that situation. And this goes on, you have to worry about so many persons.

Ken then related a similar experience, as did Pat with regard to her principal. Jack, in characteristic response, sought to turn the focus of these interchanges away from the "the other" not in the group toward the feelings of the group members themselves:

> Doesn't this put us under tremendous pressure to know that we may be doing an acceptable job with the kids when we have them, but all the time we're concerned about how the kids are going to perform when they are not with us.

And, just as characteristically during this early phase of the group, the members responded to Jack's effort at reorientation only minimally.

Also relatively early in this session, a new theme began to appear, i.e., the group members' very strong identification with their pupils. One major implication of this intense identification is the manner in which it augments the teacher's vulnerability to alienation from their school peers, e.g., if you reject my kids you reject me also. Note the following excerpt:

Ken: I told them at the beginning of the year that I picked this class because I wanted these boys. I could have taken two, I picked this one. I've seen your folders; I want every one of you in here because of who you are and what you are. I think you're the best possible class that I could have picked. No I mean it, because when they go out I'm watching. Even when they were in there the other day . . . I was looking all through the crowd to see where they were and how they were doing and you could see it. And you'd get a big wave and a big grin, you know, like I'm doing all right, and they'd play some more.

Will: You had a feeling of responsibility for them and they knew it.

Ken: It was the first time they were in there and I couldn't help it, I had to go in. I couldn't stay out.

Betty: But what happened in the situation where the teacher upstairs says to one of your boys, you may behave that way downstairs, but upstairs we don't behave like that.

Ken: Password for today—the kid looked at her and he said, you're a sack of gopher guts.

Helen: What?

Ken: That's just what he said to her as soon as she said it to him. It struck me funny. Besides, I thought she deserved it, probably . . . I don't think it was fitting to say to any child. Not the tone and not the way it came over, I wouldn't. I don't think it was fair to anybody.

Jack: So you're saying that when that message is communicated you know, you can do it down there but not up here, it's really what it does to us as much as what it does to the kids. The kids may be reacting, but we're certainly reacting to it also.

Ken continued this line of thought, emphasizing its loneliness dimension (e.g., she is a regular teacher, it's a regular school), and while indirectly revealing much about himself, he took care to consistently place himself in the best possible light, never spoke directly about his own feelings and, when the latter were pointed out to him, he bent his efforts toward justifying or explaining them away. Mary, Barbara and Helen all provided examples of analogous experiences with other teachers; and the group, in this manner, once again rallied around a topic in a universalizing, cohesiveness-enhancing manner.

Heinicke and Bales (1953) have demonstrated that "crisis-recovery" cycles are characteristic of problem solving groups. Similar wave-like movements began to be discernible about half-way through this second session. Minimally, but noticeably, minor peaks of openness about their own feelings appeared among the long troughs of pupil-centeredness, as the following interchanges illustrate:

Jack: I think all of us have had this kind of a message conveyed to us about the kids that we're working with, and what is it about the message that makes us so angry? I mean, one factor certainly is the fact that we can't respond. You know, they don't stay around for a discussion, it's a hit and run which is, as Betty says, frustrating . . . But beyond that, what is it about that communication that gets us?

Betty: It's just the complete lack of understanding.

Ken: Plus they're demeaning your student.

Betty: And she's also putting little value on what you are doing. I mean, you're just a babysitter.

Ken: That's what I don't like.

Barbara: They're not looking at you as a professional but rather, gee, you're a good egg for doing this.

Ken: They're saying something even more powerful about the kid.

Even within this sample of minimal openness, it is of interest to compare Betty's and Ken's comments. [As noted earlier, the latter was, more than any other group member, the group's driving force for maintaining pupil-centeredness.] Betty, in contrast, rapidly emerged as the most emotionally open and, perhaps interpersonally sensitive group member. Both Ken and Betty frequently assumed the role of "leader's helper," picking up a theme suggested by Jack or Will and asking the other group members questions around this theme. For Ken, the questions moved the group toward pupil concerns, while Betty clearly aided the leaders in weaning the group toward focus upon itself.

As noted earlier, the professional loneliness of the group members involved alienation from a variety of types of persons within the school culture—principal, social workers and other teachers. Their primary identification within the school setting was with their own pupils. Yet this, too, functioned for some of the group members as yet another, and perhaps even more telling, source of loneliness and interpersonal isolation. As Jack aptly stated it:

> Aren't we now putting together what we had started to discuss earlier . . . how little other people in the school understand about what we're doing with kids. And now we're talking about the likely possibility that many of the kids we are working with don't see what we're doing any more clearly than some of the other staff members. . .

A final theme of this second session is worth noting. At the beginning of this chapter we pointed out that in the third or New Problem Solving phase of the group, much emphasis was placed upon relating within-group and outside-of-group events. During this second session, i.e., near the beginning of the group's first phase, a substantial portion of the discussion of out-group events (happenings at school, etc.) did in fact relate to in-group behaviors but, because of the rudimentary nature of the group's development at this point, the connecting of the two classes of events was not made explicit by the group leaders. Concretely, nothing was made at this point in time of the fact that Ken's explicit apprehension over being observed in class and his stated need to assume an authoritarian stance in his class represented the same kinds of defensiveness and resistance to openness he was displaying within the teacher group.

The session concluded with a structuring statement by the group leaders during which the group members agreed to present, in turn, what each felt to be a significant "teacher-pupil relationship incident." Noteworthy in this structuring is the manner in which it reflected our feeling that the members would move toward personal openness not as a function of being told to do so (by structuring) but, instead, by experiencing an increasingly safe and cohesive group climate. The structuring, therefore, sought to have the members provide material which could be used by the group leaders to, in effect, "teach" openness in situations rather than explicitly requesting that they focus in depth upon themselves.

Session 3.   The Cases Begin

In overview, this session provided an accentuation and further development of most of the major themes which had emerged during the earlier two sessions. Mary presented her "case" and the rest of the group, including Will, responded to her presentation in an almost singularly pupil-centered manner. Jack, in characteristic contrast, did not meet the group at its level but, instead, pursued efforts toward shifting to a relationship focus. Loneliness reemerged in both old and new guises. Within-group cohesiveness continued to build.

As noted above, Mary began the meeting with a lengthy presentation of one of her pupils. Her calling him a "case" and her statements viewing him as almost object-like (e.g., "I find him very interesting") capture well the distancing quality of her presentation. As her statement continued, Jack sought to elicit her feelings about her interactions with the pupil but, as the following excerpt illustrates, several group members and Will combined to largely thwart this attempt.

Jack: Mary, you started your description of this youngster, what's his name?

Mary: Bob.

Jack: Bob, by saying that at the beginning of the year you found him very . . .

Mary: Very trying.

Jack: Very trying and you said something else. You said very unlikable. And then you immediately said you hate to say it.

Mary: I did at the time. When I found him unlikable and I felt guilty for it. He was so aggressive, verbally so aggressive.

Barbara: And yet, no curse words.

Mary: No, just constant going at it and leading the others on. And the others would always end up at each other's throats because of this one who would sit back and just do the talking.

Will: Was his language sophisticated when he was after another person?

Mary: Fairly, fairly.

Jack: Did his behavior have something to do with your reaction, are they separate?

Mary: His behavior. . .

Jack: You said he was verbally aggressive, but on the other hand, you said you found him unlikable and you hated to admit it, but you found him that way, it was a fact.

Mary: I think I had to pretty well, because I was so conscious of it.

Will: Was it his behavior? Is he grotesque in appearance?

Mary: No, no and after you get used to him and he quiets down, he's very likable . . . You're new in a class too. He's there as a person who is just making everything more complicated. He's setting people up at each other's throats and sitting back and chuckling. You know, egging them on, and it's just . . .

Barbara: You're sitting there handling it.
Mary: Right.
Ken: He takes advantage of everybody.
Mary: He does, he manipulates people beautifully.
Ken: You too?
Mary: Do I, oh, does he manipulate me, ah (pause) he did for a while.
Jack: Of course you could see it but you were powerless to . . .
Mary: Until I figured out how to keep him from doing it, I had to figure out how to do it.
Ken: Just before you go on, what about the drug, the drug effect?
Mary: I don't know what he's on now, he'd been on dexadrine. . .

It is worth noting in the foregoing interactions that, in addition to the successful overall thwarting of Jack's push toward relationship-centeredness, there was some minimal reappearance of the wave-like sequence of openness and closedness to relationship concerns evident also in the second group meeting. Similar wave-like behavior may be discerned in this session within the verbalizations of a given member. For example, early in the session, Ken for the first time explored his feelings in a fairly open manner—probably because the group as a whole was seen as minimally safer by him and perhaps also because of the encouragement to do so provided him by Betty. Later in the session, however, the wave had clearly receded and his distance from himself was as great as ever. Note the following excerpts illustrating, respectively, his openness and closedness.

Ken: . . . if there is something irritating about a child I start to wonder how much good I'm doing that child, or how effective I am. On some levels he drives me wild.
Mary: That's the way I felt at first.
Ken: And when I'm . . . I wonder like when I'm talking to him, I'm sending messages that I don't like him or I don't like what he's doing or it's irritating.
Betty: What do you do when you get this? I've gotten the feeling you just can't stand him, period, you know, and he's there tomorrow morning. What do you do?
Ken: Sometimes I tell him that.

These comments, and Ken's immediately following development of this theme in which he related his reactions to a pupil to his own childhood, contrast markedly with a sequence taking place later in the session. As the following excerpt illustrates, Mary's very open comment regarding the human qualities demanded of teachers causes Ken to, in a sense, run to developing the idea of "the teacher versus the person" as well as a host of pupil-centered, teacher-excusing comments.

Mary: I just felt as a teacher, as the type of teacher I am, I'm not entitled to go into a classroom and dislike anyone. You just can't function this way, and yet you know that you're human and you will. And I think the worst part was it did sneak up on me. All of a sudden it just dawned on me, I dislike this kid. And the guilt feelings were so tremendous until I forced myself to be so patient that actually it just went over my head.

Ken: Another side to your question. If you go in and figure well, as the teacher, now that's one thing and the answer is probably in the book for a method. When you start saying as the teacher that's one thing, but as a person, that's another.

Jack: They are different?

Ken: Yes.

Ken then continued this theme, elaborating in detail the differences between "the teacher" and "the person who teaches" and in this manner touched once again upon the most fundamental concept underlying this group, i.e., our effort to move in the direction of making "the teacher" and "the person" one and the same.

A final comment on wave-sequences or phase movements during this session seems appropriate before returning to its other themes. The group entered, near the end of the session, another crisis-recovery cycle. Ken responded to its labeling by drawing a parallel between the group's and his class's phasing or cycles, once again illustrating the manner in which group and classroom events are mutually reflective and provide the opportunity for in-group to out-group comparisons and learning by the group members.

Jack: Could we kind of ask ourselves how it is that we're now talking about this particular topic? I'm sitting here trying to reconstruct . . . how we got to this particular junction. Is it a breather? I wondered if I was the only one who felt that way.

Ken: We're always structuring.

Jack: In what way?

Helen: I'm not reacting as completely as we were doing before now; I'm still back there anyway.

Ken: I'm still thinking on the other level.

Jack: Kind of digesting.

Mary: Yes, and you can only do that, and then you can hike up again.

Jack: I kind of felt that way too.

Ken: This happens in the room too . . . when you meet a child who comes up and you're in this kind of bind that you were talking about before. When that incident is over the whole room goes down. All of a sudden you've got the perfect room because they know it and you know it and it's been up there and it's back down again. And everybody is content that you sit there breathing easy for about a day.

Mary, Barbara and Betty all responded to Ken's comment by providing examples of similar events in their classrooms—thus once again rallying around a topic, sharing common experiences and frustrations, and, more generally, augmenting the group's growing sense of cohesiveness. The manner in which Jack sought to encourage this augmentation of cohesiveness, as well as the group members' growing willingness to look at themselves and their relationships with pupils is illustrated by the following interaction which occurred halfway through the session.

Barbara: I don't feel I have a relationship with this child at all that I can use to his benefit or that I can use at all. I work with him on a very superficial basis.

Jack: Have some of the rest of you, several have been nodding heads in agreement, do you have kids who have the same kind of impact on you?

Pat: What seems to me has been running through the conversation is that kids make you angry when you feel you can't handle them. And that brick wall . . . it's theirs but it's also very much yours. Once you begin to feel that you can handle this child and you have your finger on a few things that you can go on, I think then you begin to like the child. This is the way I felt with Arthur . . . this kid was all over the room running across the bookcases. He was out more than he was in. I thought, you know, I can't stand him, he's driving me nuts. And when I thought it through and thought of ways to handle him, you know, you're getting a little gratification and you're getting feedback and you think, he's not so bad, you know, I like him a lot.

Helen: You're right, when you feel you're ineffective with the child. . .

Thus the group progressed. While most of the session was devoted to pupil management per se, with much direct advice giving, the teachers grew discernably in their willingness to "publicly" examine their personal contributions to their classroom interactions.

Session 4.   Helen on the Grill

The several group themes present in earlier sessions continued to progress during this meeting, i.e., wave-like sequences of openness and closedness, cohesiveness-enhancement, advice-giving, and so forth. The major emphasis remained pupil-centered. Two new themes did emerge, however, and while both were unpleasant for the group to begin dealing with, the very fact that the group was able to involve itself in such materials spoke well for its continuing development. The first such theme involved yet another dimension of teacher loneliness, and grew out of Helen's "case" presentation much of whose focus dealt with interpersonal difficulties she experienced with the parents of one of her pupils. The second newly emerging theme involved a within-group phenomenon, namely the manner in which the members constituted themselves into what Bach (1954) has termed a "peer court" and subjected Helen to rather considerable and intense grilling regarding her handling of the problem situation being focused upon. While this grilling was unpleasant for Helen, and may have even resulted in increasing the apprehension of those group members yet to present their "case," it did amply demonstrate that the group had begun to move beyond the "sweetness" stage of cohesiveness development toward a level of intermember attraction and security in which open and active disagreement was possible.

Helen opened this session with an extended description of her current problems with a pupil, much of this description dealing with the ways in which positive changes in the classroom behavior of the pupil were undone or negated by what Helen viewed as the malignant influence of the boy's mother. However, while the manifest focus of this presentation was on the pupil-parent-teacher triad, its latent theme was clearly Helen's intense frustration and anger toward the mother. Note the following excerpt:

> Will: I get a feeling you feel responsible for the child's life outside.
> Helen: At this point I feel very responsible for it.
> Will: Because you caused him to get into this trouble outside of school or bring down the wrath of his mother and everyone around him more or less?
> Helen: Yes, I do feel this.

As the group had done in earlier sessions, several members stated experiences similar to Helen's and the group was then "off and running" in a dispersed discussion involving pupil management advice-giving. Teacher role limitations were somewhat abstractly examined and, in general during the first third of the session, Jack's efforts to bring the group's focus more directly upon their own feelings were unsuccessful. Of special interest during this segment, however, are the several instances during which Betty also sought to initiate a teacher-orientation or a relationship-orientation into the group's interactions, e.g., her question to Helen: "Where do we draw the lines where teacher leaves off and Gary (the pupil) begins," and her comment later to Helen that "I couldn't help but feel earlier that you really felt responsible for what he does once he leaves you, which carried with it immense potential for guilt." Perhaps it was partly because of Betty's empathic assistance when combined with that offered by Jack, that Helen was able to communicate as openly as she did about her feelings midway through this session, as the following sequences illustrate:

Jack:	In line with what Ken was asking, in a sense the youngster is punishing you. Isn't that right? In other words, you planned and plotted and schemed. You got him to do certain things but it's not working out the way you hoped so you're getting it from that end. And now as Betty and Ken say, you're also getting it from mother.
Will:	But I think it's just like she says, she's acting just like the parent does who is defensive.

And a few moments later:

Ken:	What do you think would happen if when she called you and told you what he did at home you said, "so what?"
Barbara:	What do you want me to do about it, the question is what can *you* do about it?
Helen:	Well, I didn't. I didn't know how to handle that phone conversation.
Jack:	Did it make you angry?
Helen:	It made me uncomfortable. Yes, it made me angry.
Jack:	Ken, doesn't your question reflect a certain level of anger that you have about this?
Ken:	Yes, that and plus.
Helen:	There's a limit. She (the mother) is inflicting the responsibility into all areas.
Ken:	And if you refuse to accept it, what happens?
Barbara:	She goes to a social worker.
Betty:	Inflicting responsibility, wow; Inflicting right at the heart.
Helen:	You're not helping me.
Ken:	No, I think you have to just accept it.
Helen:	Accept what?

Ken: Accept all the responsibilities she's given you.

Betty: I wonder if she's uncomfortable with the amount of ego he takes home every night, and she needs a little back herself.

While this latter excerpt illustrates the manner in which empathy engenders openness, its last few interchanges signal the beginnings of a sense of being pressed experienced by Helen. Betty, Barbara, and in particular Ken, pursued this active grilling of Helen more fully in the immediately following interchanges:

Helen: I don't quite know how to handle what's coming next because of all this.

Betty: Where do you leave off and he begins?

Helen: I'm just plain cutting off with him now.

Betty: Is that saying anything to you?

Helen: No.

Ken: Do you think that child could do anything on his own right now?

Helen: Well, he is doing things on his own.

Ken: Without your influence?

Helen: Well, you can't say without my influence because I'm there. I don't know how much is my influence and . . . it has to be my influence.

Ken: Can you cut off, and if he gets in trouble outside the classroom. Suppose he comes down and he gets into trouble with me or something, or down to my room.

Barbara: Then he'd have to handle it.

Ken: Would you come and see me? Or would you tell him to go down, you're in it, you get out of it.

Helen: Usually when that problem comes with a child—if there is a problem—it's not the teacher.

Ken: Would you tell him how to get out of it?

Helen: I would tell him to go back and see you and how he should handle himself, not what to say.

Ken: All right, but you can pretty well depend on what the handling is going to be like, would you just say to him all right you're in it, then leave him?

Helen: I'd say yes, he'd have to go back.

This staccato-like interaction continued for several minutes—unpleasant for Helen but symptomatic of growing group ability to stop pulling punches. Throughout this interaction Betty sought to elicit personal involvement or focus upon teacher feelings.

Betty: If at some level you feel as responsible as you've indicated tonight for this boy's behavior, there must be some reciprocal feeling on his part at some level. What happens if he doesn't do as you would have him do? It's like a mother who feels responsible for everything her child does, and the child at some level is fearful of doing wrong, even to the point maybe that it would kill the mother. Could this be what is hanging up the clarity with which you see the boy now?

Helen: I haven't been thinking of it on that level.

And a few moments later:

Betty: How do you feel when he's absent?
Helen: He's never absent. He has three miles to walk and he walked it in subfreezing weather.
Betty: That's what helped me check how much I felt.
Jack: In what ways, Betty?
Betty: When he's absent, you know, where is the rest of me?
Jack: You mean sometimes you miss you?

Thus we find in this interaction not only growing measures of openness and self-disclosure, but evidence that teacher identification with a pupil may be so marked as to make them almost appear transitive in the teacher's eyes. But of course, no group member's behavior can be described unidimensionally. Thus, Betty, as the following sequence demonstrates, at times augmented Helen's sense of being pressured with a sequence of direct questions.

Betty: What can he do that's acceptable in the classroom when he's very angry. He's going to get angry because he has all this underlying hostility. You said before, Gary, if you have to be angry you can go outside, but there must be some acceptable way in which he can do it in the room.
Helen: He can show anger through verbal expression.
Betty: All right, is that the limit now?
Helen: Yes.
Ken: How loud in front of everybody else?
Helen: Well, it's usually to me.
Betty: Can he pound the desk?
Helen: Yes, but what he does right now is goes inside of his desk.
Betty: Okay, but what's acceptable for Gary in expressing anger right now in the room.
Helen: Verbal.
Betty: Verbal at your desk?
Helen: Verbal at the desk.
Betty: Yes but that's not pounding your desk. Okay, so if he pounds the desk, what happens.
Helen: He hasn't done this.
Betty: Okay.

Helen: He has cut off all this behavior.

Betty: But if he lets out anger in any other way, kicking the desk or pounding somebody?

Helen: All right, if he kicks over he goes to the door and I talk to him at the door.

Betty: Is sometimes the question maybe I'm not letting him let out enough here at school so it backs up and lets out at home. Does that ever come to your mind?

Helen: Well, that's what came to my mind briefly when she said he's intolerable at home. And I was thinking, no problems here anymore. . . She said, what are you doing to him that he has to let off? And I said, well, maybe this is what's happening and I didn't proceed because everything was so smooth at school.

We wonder what expectations the several sequences such as the above aroused in Barbara and Pat during the first two thirds of this session. Neither had presented their "cases" yet nor essentially participated in "probing" Helen, and Helen had received relatively little support from either group leader during this part of the session.

Toward the end of the session, the leaders and the other group members became somewhat more supportive of Helen, and this was reflected not only in her behavior but, for the first time during the session, Mary openly discussed her feelings.

Helen: This involvement, I don't know, I've come to the conclusion that you do your worst job when you're so involved.

Mary: Oh, I know that. I went through it myself last year. I felt that it was the worst year of my life, like the worst job I ever did in anything because I was too involved.

Betty: Helen, you mean the awareness that you were perhaps involved. You were on the witness stand when the mother called you.

Helen: Right.

Ken: Or when they don't need it anymore.

Helen: Right.

Betty: Why am I on the witness stand?

Helen: Up to that time I didn't feel that at all.

Jack: But it was there, is that what you're saying?

Helen: Right.

Jack: Mary, why was it the worst year of your life?

Mary: Oh, I just felt like at the end of the year I had accomplished absolutely nothing because I'd become so involved. I just felt with the kids too much, too much. I was too busy understanding the way they felt and feeling sorry for them and doing this for them and that for them and getting nothing accomplished, absolutely nothing.

Session 5. The Rise and Fall of Resistance

The major trends apparent in earlier sessions were in evidence during this fifth meeting, but in highly exaggerated form. The group's level of pupil-centered resistiveness reached a new high during most of the session, but a new low toward its end. Jack displayed greater sensitivity to the members' needs and feelings than was true in earlier meetings. Will displayed even less. As we focus on the details of this session, the relatedness of member resistance versus openness to the behavior of the group's leaders will be apparent.

The session began with a brief series of tension release interactions in which the effects of the grilling Helen had received the week before were causatively central. The members were seeking to reduce the reheightened disclosure anxiety occasioned by Helen's treatment, thus once again demonstrating that it is what the group members *experience*, rather than the verbal information provided them by the group's leaders, which serves as the major influence structuring their group-relevant expectancies.

Pat then presented, at considerable length, a problem classroom situation involving two of her pupils. At no point during her presentation was even passing mention made of Pat the person, her feelings or her needs. As the presentation continued, Will entered in. Note in the excerpt below how his contribution served its characteristic purpose of augmenting a sense of universalization in the group but, equally characteristically, failed to reorient Pat's focus toward herself to any degree whatsoever. This is the case even though, as the excerpt illustrates, Pat is personally very highly involved in the situation discussed.

Will: We had two like that at one point and it seemed like we tried everything, everything. We talked with them together and alone over several months and we finally made it through the end of the year, but these two hated each other.

Helen: I had this same situation. It's like you can't find any way to deal with it.

Pat: Yes, and if they were on similar levels you could deal with it in a better way. But with Roger nothing seems to be meaningful to him . . . It's gotten really worse the past two weeks. They see each other in the halls . . . They yell at each other in the cafeteria. Roger was going out and Arthur was going in. I'm going to get you later frost turd, and he said, Oh, yeah, jackass, I'll get you too. And

I thought, oh, right in the middle of the cafeteria. And I disappeared.

Pat's presentation continued for about a third of the session, with all of Jack's efforts towards a relationship focus being thwarted by the group members and by Will. Since so much of the latter's group behavior was member-like, Jack apparently decided to respond to his co-leader as if he were "just a group member" and sought to reorient *Will's* pupil-centeredness such that Will would discuss *his* feelings about *his* relationships with pupils. The following interchange demonstrates that Jack's efforts were at first fully resisted and then, at best, only temporarily successful as Will departed only momentarily from his exclusive pupil focus.

Will: Two kids I knew about, one kid had a tremendous time learning. It was proved that he had some brain damage. And especially math, he really just couldn't do it. And this other little character was really quick. He used to do all these numbers real quick and then laugh at Tommy. And these two, you know, they were at each other just like this.

Jack: Were you involved in this situation?

Will: Not in the classroom too much although I observed it in the classroom. I got many of the after effects. . . . The boy who had difficulty even when he could get it would not do his work because the other kid's mother used to drive them both home at night and therefore the smart kid had to wait for him every night and, oh, just amazing ways of getting at each other.

Jack: Theoretically you were a dispassionate observer here but you seem to have gotten involved. You weren't even in the classroom but apparently this had some impact on you.

Will: I had the same kind of feeling that, about these two, that there was a tremendous intensity of feeling between the two kids. And it went very deep and what the one kid was doing represented a great deal to the other kid, and so . . .

Jack: What did it do to you?

Will: What did it do to me?

Jack: Yes.

Will: It frustrated me. It absolutely frustrated me because this one kid couldn't learn like the other. . . This kid who couldn't learn came from a high achieving family. His father was a professor at the University and he knew how to hurt a guy.

Jack's further reorienting efforts were thwarted consistently, but in varying ways. In the first example below, he succeeded very briefly in eliciting a self-focusing response from Betty—who was the major member opening in the wall of resistance during this session—but Helen then proceeded to wean the group back to an exclusive pupil concern. In the second example, a heroic effort by Jack was bluntly and simply ignored, perhaps demonstrating that the more forceful or frontal a leader's attack on resistiveness, the greater the resistance it engenders.

Jack: Having behavior like this hang over your head, over the course of months, it must be extremely difficult day after day when it's so predictable.

Betty: It's so draining.

Helen: It's extremely difficult. I haven't found any way of working with it. Neither of the boys can be approached. One of them is the one I mentioned. The psychiatrist said hands off. And the other one I mentioned a couple of weeks ago. It starts out with so and so is a slob and then it goes so and so is a whore and it progressively gets worse and worse.

Jack: Well, I feel like I need some clarification, perhaps we do as a group. In discussing individual youngsters like this are we discussing individual youngsters for what kinds of purposes? In other words, as I listen to our conversation tonight we seem to be vacillating between talking about specific techniques and interventions and then kinds of feelings we have about very difficult situations. And then some people have started to generalize to even broader kinds of issues like the issue of are we in fact talking about teacher potency. What does a situation like this do to your own self image as somebody who is in control of the group? I'm wondering if this would be the time to clarify our use of one case to start off with?

Barbara: What were the results from our tests?

The group's high level of resistiveness continued. Jack consistently pulled, poked and prodded toward teacher-centeredness, receiving occasional help from Betty or Will—but generally without notable success. Toward the end of the session, however, Jack's tenacity yielded handsome dividends as the group rapidly moved from high to very low levels of resistiveness, as the following separate excerpts illustrate.

Jack: Well, if I were the teacher in this instance, I'd be very mad at Roger for doing this to Arthur.

Pat: Maybe I am, but I haven't admitted it to myself. I think a lot of times I'm mad at him for what it does to the whole class, and how we can't get going.

Jack: I mean you have good reason.

Will: Yes, absolutely, forty-five minutes out of every two hours.

Barbara: Have you ever told him you are angry?
Pat: I think the way I talk to him, he knows.

*   *   *

Betty: If you could remove anything from your classroom right
          now, to make it more comfortable for you to live and do a
          better job, what would it be?
Pat: Roger.
Betty: Are you saying you can't tolerate Roger, as he is now?
Pat: I'll be completely honest about my feelings about Roger.
          I can tolerate a lot from Roger, but he's the kind of kid
          that gives you so much that suddenly you're just up to here
          and you want to say goodbye Roger.

*   *   *

Pat: I think one good thing that has come out of this is that
          I think I really need to examine my feelings toward Roger,
          you know, I know that this is the place for him and I
          think he can be helped in this, but he's really taxing, as
          far as taking a lot out of you.

Session 6.   The Missing Leader

As has been noted several times earlier, the vast majority of times at
which a group member openly examined his own feelings or contribution to a problem situation were primarily a function of Jack's leadership efforts in this direction. Jack was absent from this sixth session
and there existed in the group no countervailing force to move the
group away from the pupil-centered stance it still naturalistically tended
to assume. In later sessions, when the group culture had more fully
matured, Jack played a less vital role in its movement toward a relationship focus. At that later point, such members as Betty were frequently able to assume such a leadership function. This was not true
of the present session, however, and it was almost totally lacking in any
progress toward group goals.

It was Barbara's turn to present at this session and, at first glance,
her presentation bore the same pupil-centered focus as had other
"cases." Yet, perhaps the group's past sessions had begun to leave their
mark. The excerpt which follows is the opening of Barbara's presentation. While its manifest content is John, the pupil, note the indirect
ways in which Barbara reveals information about herself, e.g., such
diverse personal feelings as confusion, enjoyment, investment in John,
and a deep sense of frustration.

Barbara: I don't know why I'm going to present this . . . I guess the main reason is because with each one of us that has presented so far we've had a question about the child . . . and I guess this is really what I feel about John. The thing that really confuses me about John is how much I enjoy working with him, yet how much he has changed, he's constantly changing every day. I never quite know what to expect with John. . . . The reason I'm trying so hard to describe him is because in a lot of cases he's a child I don't know how to describe. When you first look at John you could look at him as a normal child almost, yet when you get down under him there is so much there that he just will not let you touch. And what everyone who's working with John right now is saying, which I'm saying too, is I can't reach John, I don't feel I'm reaching him.

As noted earlier, no group resource existed during most of this session which could provide the requisite sensitivity and respond to *Barbara's* needs and feelings. And thus the group quite rapidly drifted off into hearing Barbara out in a discussion at length of various dimensions of John—the pupil. When Will entered the discussion, after about ten minutes had elapsed, it was simply as another group member seeking factual clarification.

Barbara: Well, he was beaten quite severely, and I think this was classic with John. At about five years old he wanted to write a thank you note to his grandmother. The first time he wrote it they said it wasn't . . . spelled right or too sloppy. So they slapped him and made him write it again. This time John wrote it completely backward. This is at five years old, wrote it completely backwards. They hit him.
Ken: Backwards?
Barbara: Backwards.
Ken: Bottom to top, that kind of thing?
Barbara: Right. The next time they hit him with a strap, he wrote half of it backwards. The father hit him with a chain.
Will: This is his real father?

When the group, instead of directly aiding Barbara's "flight from herself" by joining her in flight, sought to force her to reveal her feelings, they obtained equally pupil-centered results. Stated otherwise, the group was insensitive to Barbara's feelings usually by agreeing with her to ignore them, but sometimes were insensitive via a forced confrontation—which resulted in an equally speedy "flight from herself" into a focus on John. Note the following illustration:

Will: Wait a minute, we've asked Barbara a lot of questions.
Betty: Mary has one on the floor I think.
Mary: What makes you like him?
Will: Okay.
Mary: You know, all of this behavior sounds like what do I do
          with this kid? I would feel like hitting my head against
          a wall, and yet you like him!
Barbara: I'm trying . . . if I could find and really verbalize John's
          strengths. Maybe this is what I'm trying to get at, because
          I feel he's got them. This is a kid that yesterday really
          wanted to try and he did it, he did it for the whole day,
          and he was happy with it. But he can't hold it.

And again, a few moments later:

Will: Tell us your feelings, I think that's the way it has to go.
Barbara: I feel that he feels physically safe when you can put on . . .
          lately when I have been able to put my arm around him . . .
          he just glues himself to you like please protect me. But
          the thing is, the way his family right now is showing affec-
          tion to this child through a poodle whom John has to take
          care of, whom he hates.

These excerpts, when considered in conjunction with the openness
following many of Jack's comments in earlier sessions, pointedly illustrates that personal feelings are *not* revealed on demand. Group members must *experience* a sense of being understood, a sense of moving
arm in arm with others in the group. It is, as Truax and Carkhuff
(1967) have repeatedly demonstrated, warmth and accurate empathy
which engender openness, and not pointed requests to disclose.

As noted, Will not infrequently offered the group direct questions,
much as the other group members were prone to do. He behaved as
"just another member" in other ways. Leader spontaneity does not
appear to be an appropriate leadership behavior. That is, while it is
indeed often worthwhile, and at times crucial, for group leaders to
share *their* personal feelings with the group, such sharing should *always*
be preceded by the leader asking himself whether such sharing is in
the group's best interest or only his own. If the former, leader disclosure
should certainly be encouraged; if the latter, quite the contrary seems
appropriate. In the excerpt which follows, the latter does seem to be
the case in that (a) Will's own sense of being threatened was revealed,
and (b) no constructive use was made by him of his revelation to the
group. If anything, his comments serve the purpose of moving Barbara

further away from exploration of her own feelings—as the discussion led to an agreeable but goal-irrelevant process of Will taking both himself and Barbara off the emotional hook.

Will: Is the father threatening?

Barbara: Oh, the father, to me? No.

Will: Is he a threatening kind of person?

Barbara: To John?

Will: To meet?

Barbara: No, because he hides behind his glasses. He can't threaten you, he's hiding.

Ken: So he's hiding behind something and you have to talk to him.

Will: He's not threatening to you?

Barbara: No.

Will: That's funny, he's very threatening to me. I talked to him for 45 minutes on the phone last fall and he talked to me about what the hell is the matter with this kid. Almost as if we were trying to punish the kid. And we had to talk to him. I had to talk to him about the fact that the kid was exhibiting problems and so forth and finally, it was very difficult, I got him to accept the idea that special classes were probably necessary. But I felt that he had very little insight into this and that he was very threatened by the whole idea. And he's a big guy behind those sun glasses and it's almost as if, you know, if you don't agree with me, I'll punch you right in the nose. Don't you feel that way?

Barbara: No, I didn't at all.

Will: I don't know, maybe it's because you're a woman.

Barbara: Well, he . . . well, maybe so.

At the beginning of our discussion of this session we noted the several instances of rather clear, if indirect, statements of feeling latent in Barbara's presentation. This general notion, that one's own needs and feelings are revealed when another person is focused upon, was equally true for the other teacher's statements about various pupils. For example, our earlier comments on Ken have suggested a rather defensive individual who prefers a world arranged in neat, cognitive packages. Children presented by the other group members were diagnosed by him, looked at from a distance, viewed as objects to control —but rarely empathized with. Emotional involvement with a pupil one suspects, raised the spectre of the possibility that Ken would have to look more closely at his own feelings. And this he found difficult to do indeed. Note the following interchange between Ken and Will, an interchange illustrating both Ken's orientation and, additionally, providing further examples of Will's directiveness.

Will: Why don't you like him?
Ken: I'm getting nervous talking about him.
Will: All right, but why don't you? Why don't you like him?
Ken: I can't understand it.
Will: Barbara keeps talking about the fact that she likes him and you don't like him. Now why don't you like him?
Ken: I haven't seen any strong point.
Betty: She hasn't given us the basis for her liking him.
Will: Well, that's what I mean, but why don't you like him?
Ken: Well, I can't center on anything that seems to be the problem with the child. His home life is a keg of dynamite. His father is hiding behind sun glasses and coming out at different people and then going back behind them again. . . I don't know what he is capable of . . . how badly he will act, what he will do . . . there's no real way to deal with him. There's no area that I've seen that you can keep zeroing in on and build on.
Betty: Wait, a minute, are you saying there isn't or we haven't?
Ken: I haven't seen any yet.
Barbara: Any real what, Ken?
Ken: Handle, there's no real handle. He's most probably going to get worse. He's going to move away, you can't control that. . . He's going to get worse.
Barbara: Perhaps.
Ken: And I would prefer not to deal with this kind of a child. I'd put a lot of distance between myself and him. . . .

Perhaps we can best summarize our discussion of this progressless, sixth session with the following brief excerpt. Note that it follows a full hour in which Barbara, several dozen times, expressed strong emotion toward John, always in the guise of talking about him alone. At one and the same time it is a marked opportunity for movement toward a relationship focus and a total and unequivocal rejection of this opportunity by the group.

Barbara: I think I know what you're getting to is that I'm emotionally involved with this child.
Ken: No.
Helen: No.
Barbara: And yet, I'm not at all.

Session 7.   The Group Turns Inward

This session was a major turning point in the group's development, a session in which movement toward focus on teacher needs and feelings was as great as was the movement away from these areas in the preceding session. The content of this turning inward was the group's looking at itself—its resistiveness, goals, cohesiveness, roles, etc. The major impetus for this open and introspective development was provided by Jack and Betty, the latter blooming in this session as an immensely sensitive quasi-group leader. It is not clear whether it was Jack and Betty's behavior alone which caused this favorable and rather dramatic group refocus, or whether the vacuousness of the preceding session was also responsible. Most likely both these factors and all preceding sessions were necessary preconditions, that is the earlier opportunities for the group to develop the requisite sense of growing trust. In any event, this session was indeed a crossroads. The group chose a new path and never turned back from it in subsequent sessions, all of which involved greater openness, cohesiveness and ability to look at oneself than had the first six group meetings.

The session began with a rather general discussion in the group of some of the tests* they had been requested to take by Jack and Will, a discussion which very rapidly led to the following focus on within-group events.

Jack: The three of you are reacting to what Will said. Will said that if we do start talking about the forms, it will get personal. Helen, you responded very quickly by saying we already have. Barbara and Betty kind of concurred. Is this your perception of what we've been doing so far? Or the direction that we're moving in?
Helen: Yes, we've hit pretty hard and have tossed a lot of things up, I think.
Barbara: Yes, we have.
Helen: Really down on a gut level.

The group generally agreed that "things were getting personal," leading Betty to offer the following resistance—identifying and cohesiveness—augmenting comment.

Betty: I get the feeling that those of us around the table have not been certainly overly sensitive to the feelings of the person who is presenting. We've gone our way, we throw things at him and we live on the line that they live on every day. Why aren't we more sensitive in the way we phrase things? The second point is that speaking for myself, is that as colleagues in the field there is a kind of assumption that you

* The nature and results of the project's testing program are discussed in the Appendix.

know we're not against you. We are working together. And whatever we say we throw out trying to get at something below what the level upon which we're now speaking, the point being that a role has become established in the group of present and then boom, all these things come at you. Nobody has set it up formally but it has happened.

We might characterize the foregoing statement, using Bach's (1954) terms, as a "within-group inspection." These are observations by group members of the dynamic interplay of forces within the group. Many more such comments occurred in this and later sessions, and their importance is considerable. In a manner not unlike that of a T-group or sensitivity group, the members made increasing use of these within-group inspections, especially in later sessions, for purposes of better understanding out-group (especially at school) events. This process of in-group to out-group generalization is one we will focus on heavily later in this section. We simply note it here since Betty's comment seems to provide one of our first major examples of an important within-group inspection. This within-group focus continued:

Betty: I know at times I've asked particular questions knowing that they are pressure creating, not to put a person on the spot and force them into a corner, but to push us all to another level of thinking, assuming that it was completely understood that this is one of the reasons. I may be completely wrong.

Jack: Okay, what might you be wrong about?

Betty: Well, assuming that we're safe enough to do this.

Jack: But you said presumably we're meeting for what?

Betty: To pursue different levels of looking at teacher decisions, teacher relationship with kids, aren't we?

Jack: Okay.

Betty: We were talking about what it is that happens in a classroom between teacher and child.

Jack: You raised the most important question, of course, the reason for our meeting.

Betty: And certainly those that don't present, because of the way the structure of the group has evolved really, those of us not presenting seem to have a structurally safer position.

Other group members rapidly joined in with related within-group inspections:

Ken: I think sometimes even the way a question is worded is interference you build into the question . . . already has a buffer put in.

Jack: Like what, Ken?

Ken: The way a question is asked to a person, you can go right at them, you can make a question hurt. Or you can make it out for information, you can qualify it somewhat and it's really ineffective and doesn't demand an answer.

Jack: Do you think that's happened?

Ken.   I think sometimes . . . if a person has a real blind spot, and you think you see it, you'd rather not hit it. You'd, you know, ask around it.

Note that in both of the sequences above, Betty and Ken have not directed their statements to or about specific fellow members. Betty speaks of whether "the group" is safe; Ken talks of "the person's" blind spot. Thus, while they clearly are at the point of beginning to look at the group, it is still a "looking" which is rather depersonalized and cautious. This process of personalization, too, changed toward more directness as the group continued to proceed.

We noted earlier several possible reasons for the group's turning inward during this session. This process may also be characterized, because of the content of the turning inward, as in large measure consisting of an analysis of group resistance. Clinicians have long held that resistances must be dealt with as a precondition to patient progress, and we would hold much the same viewpoint for this teacher group. Yet the manner in which resistances are handled is crucial. A direct, frontal attack typically results in heightened, not diminished defensiveness. An empathetic, arm-in-arm approach in which leader and led seek in common cause to examine defenses is characteristically much more successful. In the excerpt which follows, we see Will first attempt the frontal, strong arm approach and then Jack an empathetic, arm-in-arm approach. It will be clear that the former does indeed fail; the later indeed succeeds.

Will: I think we have a great need to heal each other. I think we are doing it right now. I think we are trying to explain away the fact that it's difficult to get at our part in the damn thing that goes on with the kid. I think we talk a lot about what the kids feel and how they act and I think I've had a hell of a time trying to ask myself or others how they've gotten into it. I think you're talking about facts and all this and I'm not sure what this had to do with it.

Helen: We start with facts, but we don't always stay with facts. We've hit many issues and gone into feelings.

Barbara: We start with perceptions. . .

Will: You think I'm pushing too hard?

Helen: Towards what?
Will: Towards what I've been talking about.

*   *   *

Will: I said, she's questioning what I was talking about here. . .
           I get the feeling that you presume that I'm going too far
           with this issue of pushing on, of exploring our feelings
           in regard to how we handle the kids.
Helen: Well, I think we've been doing it, are you saying. . .
Will: That's what I mean.
Helen: Okay.
Will: As I said, I'm presuming that we haven't been doing very
           much of it. . .
Barbara: Well, you're saying so far we're going into shallow feelings,
           rather than really depth feelings of working with these kids.
           We're still hitting only the. . .
Will: I don't know if it's shallow or deep, but I wonder if there
           is enough of it. I think we do it and we get back off it
           and we go on for half an hour trying to get a few more
           facts.

In contrast, note the following sequence occurring approximately
ten minutes later, a sequence in which Jack offers the group what might
be termed "gentle empathy" and the group responds with openness.

Helen: In other words, we've all been just a little bit too polite.
Jack: Betty, would this be a time to ask are there some things
           happening within the group that might impede this kind of
           communication?
Betty: How can we find out?
Jack: I'm asking to find out, like. . .
Ken: One is a reluctance to deny the effectiveness or validity of
           that feeling. Hey, you shouldn't feel that way. And then
           you get into should. If she has a feeling on it and I have
           another one, that's not the same as hers, do I question hers
           or do I say, look, I don't feel like that, you've no right to
           feel like this.
Jack: Or do you raise your own feeling? In other words, Pat is
           saying, you've got some feeling or some concern behind your
           question.
Ken: Right.
Jack: So why can't you say that?
Ken: All right, and the reluctance came from what you said be-
           fore about this other thing. There's no right, there's no
           wrong, there's no should.
Betty: Look at the question though that comes in. How much
           do we trust our own perception?
Ken: Or how much do we respect the other guy?

*   *   *

Jack: Are we saying that when Pat presents, she lays out a problem on the table and then we begin asking questions. The questions, however, mask some of our own feelings and anxieties and concerns. We are then putting the responsibility on the presentor to kind of seek out some hidden messages.

Betty: And to relieve ourselves.

Jack: And relieve ourselves, is that what we are doing?

Pat: That's how I felt.

The group began to examine yet other dimensions of its past behavior. They talked about the sense of "being grilled" some had experienced in earlier sessions; there was much additional restructuring discussion, focusing largely on group goals; considerable focus upon leader-member relations and the issue of formality versus informality of these relationships; and considerable exploration of the anxiety which permeated the group during the sixth session. This broadly ranging within-group exploration yielded the promise that the members were likely on the road to analogous openness about their relationships with pupils. This is not to say that there were not periods of resistance during this session, but they were brief and yielded much more rapidly than during earlier sessions.

This desired openness regarding teacher-pupil relationships bloomed more fully starting with the very next session, but even in the present one there were a handful of comments such as Pat's:

Pat: I was thinking when I presented and I mentioned that Roger stayed after class every day and he (Will) said how do you feel about that? You know, for the first time it really hit me, that makes me mad! I can't go have my cigarette, that rotten kid. . .

In sum, the group turned inward and, by so doing, gained some freedom to return outward in a deeper and more meaningful manner.

Session 8.   It's O.K. to Feel

The group members' openness to exploring their own feelings continued during this session, at even deeper levels. Jack continued to function as the major catalyst for this exploration, with Will contributing relatively little. This growing openness to self was, with the continued exception of Ken, group wide. Anger, guilt, intimacy, the threat of separation and, above all, loneliness, all were revealed and examined.

The session opened with a group-wide discussion of confidentiality. Members were very much aware that the sharing of feelings in the previous session had set them on a path on which even more openness, more "personalness" might occur and, with this direction in mind, several members asked, in a sense, can we trust each other? The group answered this question affirmatively in two ways, directly with straight-forward statements of trust at this point in the session, and more consequentially, with deeper levels of openness about themselves as the session drew on. An interesting incidental revelation emerging from this discussion of confidentiality were the comments from a few of the members that they each knew teachers, not in the group, who spoke with great envy about such a group and who expressed the wish for a similar opportunity. The group's very positive reaction to this information clearly revealed its cohesiveness-enhancing effect.

An early statement by Jack summarized much of the groups' feeling about the previous session. Note the manner in which Jack's statement is also an example of when it *is* appropriate for a group leader to reveal his own feelings, in that it stimulates Barbara to reveal yet another dimension of her sense of professional loneliness.

Jack: The meeting had an impact on me and I think it did on some others and I guess what you're saying is that we did get down to bare rock in terms of talking about feelings. It did this to you, to me and some of you other folks have expressed it.

Barbara: You know, I guess it comes back almost . . . about this discussion today again brought it up that you know you can't communicate with the social worker . . . I sometimes feel in this you're really communicating with the kids. You know you can get through to them beautifully and you try to work with an adult and you run into all this role playing bit and I was just fed up to the hilt with it last week. You know . . . these kids . . . you communicate with them, then all of a sudden you start working with adults and . . . you're butting your head against a rock wall.

Lest the reader conclude that resistiveness totally disappeared, such was indeed not the case. During this session, Pat at one point complained of the group's "losing its focus," Barbara that "we (the group) suddenly took away the format," Betty spoke of disclosure discomfort, and Ken was frequently guarded. The point, however, is that such displays of resistiveness had become the exception, and no longer the rule. Openness clearly prevailed. First, anger:

Pat:　　Roger stays until 11:40. Well, how do you feel, you know, I'm angry, it makes me mad so after that I went back to school and you know Roger is hanging around and I said, Roger, I'm going to take a break and I picked up my purse and walked out. . .

　　　　*　　　　　　　*　　　　　　　*

Mary:　　I've got a boy that does that . . . it takes him ten minutes to leave the room, so I start him ten minutes before the bell but he still waits until the bell before he starts, it just doesn't work and I found myself getting so mad. . .

Then guilt:

Helen:　　Where it's a child you feel guilty because you know you want to get out and you feel you shouldn't feel this way.

　　　　*　　　　　　　*　　　　　　　*

Barbara:　　Sometimes it almost gets to be a cycle, you know, and like you say, you feel guilty about it . . . I think in dealing with these kids you feel guilty about it . . . like you've got to give every minute of every hour of every day.
Mary:　　I feel guity when I take my full lunch period.
Helen:　　I do too or when a child comes to the door and I just brush him aside. . .

And then, both intimacy and loss:

Betty:　　. . . When I was ready to accept the change that everyone was moving out, I began operating in a preparatory way with the total class, and I began to feel a definite resonance between this girl and myself about how we felt about it and the tone of—I would describe it as a counselor-camper relationship at a camp—that kind of a closeness in the sense that non-verbal communication was unquestionable. You know, a touch of the hand I'm sure meant the same thing to her as it did to me, a nod of the head, a glance, all of these—in the classroom, in the hall, everywhere. . . I didn't call the youngsters up to discuss their individual plans but this one day everybody just seemed to move up one by one to me and to talk about what it meant to them, everybody except Pam, which I'm glad because I wasn't ready to discuss it with her. When I was ready I just, I had the strong feeling, she isn't going to be able to verbalize anything about this. I thought, you know, I'll have to put it into words for her, what's going on, how you feel when you leave something like this, the kinds of things you look forward to, why this step is necessary for her at this particular time. . . . So when the day came, she was just as ready apparently that day as I was . . . (She) comes up to the table, sits down . . . so I talked with her . . . about what it meant in terms of Pam, why this move was taking place, how I saw Pam in readiness for it and so forth. And she looked at me right in the eyeballs and said, what I thought she could never say, I said do you understand and she said yes, but I don't want to leave you . . . I have confidence in you. If it had been said a week earlier I would have been completely unable to handle it. I think I would have walked out of the classroom. . . .

In addition to the marked affective openness of this session, a beginning spread was discernible in the group's leadership behavior. Prior to this session, in addition to Jack and Will, only Betty spontaneously assumed the role of catalyst or encourager of openness from other members. In the present session, however, both Mary and Pat functioned in a similar role—in each case seeking with only partial success to draw Ken out in terms of his own feelings.

Session 9.   We're Alone Together Now

The group's emotional openness continued to develop further during this session, with a variety of feelings being expressed more deeply and intensely than in previous meetings. Although it subsequently appeared to be largely unnecessary to augment the group's motivation for openness by "artificial" means, we did in a sense do this at the beginning of this and the next few group sessions by asking the members in turn to re-present the "cases" they had presented in earlier sessions. However, whereas in the earlier presentation the focus was naturalistically on the pupil, in the re-presentation the same child was to be discussed but the discussional emphasis was to be upon the teacher's feelings and the teacher-pupil relationship. In this ninth session, this task fell to Mary. Loneliness, once again, was centerstage for much of the session, but also revealed and examined were feelings of powerlessness, guilt, hostility and marked teacher identification with their pupils. Partially as a function of such shared openness, and in part due to common hostility toward and perceived threat from "regular" teachers, the group's level of cohesiveness was augmented considerably. Perhaps most salient as the keynote of this session was the manner in which group members began to *accept* their feelings as appropriate, in contrast to recent sessions in which feelings, while expressed, were more characteristically "confessed" or "admitted."

The group's emotional level of discourse, which even included Ken at some points, is illustrated by the following excerpt from early in the session:

Mary: He hasn't been cursing all year long . . . and for him I thought it was great that he started cursing because he was like this, all tensed up, and you could see him shaking all over, which he doesn't do now. Instead he just lets out a beautiful string of, you say it and he's said it. And this was good, I thought. Now it's getting to the point where I'd like to cut it down and I haven't found a way. . . That's why he irritated me today too, not just my mood. And I cannot figure out a way.

Ken: I got the same one. . . If I begin to react to a child and if they switch levels real quick on me. Or if I approach them a certain way and they outgrow it and I don't know it. All of a sudden I get frustrated. I get very angry at them. You know, cut it out. Now, we figured this way and it was working, settle down.

Barbara: Yes, stay with me.

Mary: He's ready for something new and he's not agreeing with you.

Ken: He's pulling something new on me.

Jack: What is it, what kind of thing does that do to us?

Ken: Right then?

Jack: Yes.

Ken: It's maddening, you don't know what to do. . .

Mary: It makes me feel very incompetent at times. What am I going to do. . .

This sense of powerlessness was generalized by the group members, and shortly led to a discussion, exemplified below, of the feelings of hostility which result from this lack of perceived progress.

Barbara: John is angry at me today and he says I'm going to burp in your face.

Ken: If you do, I'll smash you.

Barbara: All right, so where do we go from here?

Jack: So not only are we showing our own anger, but the kids in their own cute little ways are being very hostile.

Helen: My hostility is coming out.

Jack: So . . . who is generating that hostility? Because of our own anger? In other words, is it a reflection of the levels that the kids are on or is it really our level?

Barbara: No, it makes you look bad. It's spring, and like Helen says, your kids are all over the place and you think, if somebody walked into my room, what are they going to think I've accomplished since September.

Will: In other words you feel bad partly because of what other people think?

Barbara: Yes, the other day somebody said the kids downstairs are going wild. . .

Helen: That's why I've been locking my door lately, so nobody can come in without knocking.

These group-wide discussions of the sense of powerlessness often experienced by the group members, as well as resultant and rather diffuse feelings of hostility, were prefatory to a major group exploration of loneliness, the theme which more and more was becoming the keynote emotional focus for the group. As noted in our descriptions of earlier sessions, the loneliness theme appears to have several sources. The school principals tend to be oriented toward pupils "behaving themselves" and, at times, leave the group members feeling misunderstood, their efforts unappreciated. The school maintenance staffs have frequently complained to the teachers about the physical consequences of their pupils' behavior. The psychology and social work personnel have seemed, to our teachers, to be functioning on a different level than they. The pupils' parents have frequently been upset by pupil behavioral deterioration *and* improvement, as the family system has been forced to change. And, at frequent times, the teachers in our groups have expressed a feeling of alienation from their pupils themselves. Piled on top of these various and diverse sources of loneliness is, perhaps, the most important source of all, one's fellow teachers at school. Note the following excerpts:

Pat: You know, we get that all the time. Take that kid and shake him. Knock him up against the wall, he won't do it again. What that kid needs is a good spanking. Why do you take all that from them? They don't need it, you should see how well they behave when they get a substitute.

Will: Right.

Pat: There was no shoving in this school (they say to me). You know, my kids look at your kids when they go up and down the halls and my kids want to act like your kids in the halls. Now what's the problem here?

Will: Exactly, it sounds, that could be played in every school I've been in. . . When they tell me that, I'd like to punch them right in the mouth. I'd like to say what the hell do you think they are down there for, your pushing them up against the wall has done this to them. That's what I want to say to them.

Pat: You have to live with those teachers.

Will: I don't say that, I said that's what I'd like to say.

Jack: So, when I said before that we're feeling angry, this is. . .

Helen: That's happened to me.
Pat: Yes, I'm angry at all those other teachers.
Helen: In the auditorium . . . it was the first time I had the new kids and I was really having a difficult time and another teacher . . . I was handling it, but I wasn't handling it like regular kids. In other words, they were kneeling on the seats so they could see. And this other teacher . . . just stepped in and took over because she felt the behavior was inadequate and I wasn't handling it.
Betty: You shouldn't have taken that.
Pat: You just said the word inadequate and you hear it for six months and you finally say, my God, I must be!

*   *   *

Jack: Before we were saying that one of the problems is exposing ourselves to the kids, or just exposing ourselves. Losing control. Maybe this is one of the reasons for reluctance to give ourselves away, because we are so vulnerable.
Betty: There's an awful sense of aloneness in this bottle too.
Pat: Yes.
Jack: What do you mean, Betty?
Betty: Well, this awful kind of questioning, and there is nobody there with you.

*   *   *

Helen: You know lately I've been having dreams about my class and in these dreams I always have all the mothers in the school. And all the administration, the secretaries and the teachers. They are all sitting in my room and refusing to go and saying you're not handling it.
Jack: They are all against you is what you're saying, is that it?
Helen: That's the way it was in the dream.

*   *   *

Pat: You're being tested and watched by everyone from the janitors on up.
Betty: Like we say to the kids, there are some things you don't want to do. You know we teach reality. Well, it's sticking us in the face and we don't like it.
Jack: I don't think Sigmund Freud would hold up under this.
Barbara: You know, the thing too is that when you try to talk to other people in the field about your kids . . . they interpret it so negatively that I quit talking to people.

*   *   *

Jack: So really we're describing that we're scapegoated just like the kids, is that it?
Barbara: You've identified with them.

Jack: If we have anybody to identify with, it's with the kids, and they don't exactly want us. And here we are. Who's left if you won't take me Shorty? Who else is there to turn to?

Ken: The janitors. I'm not kidding, they come in wonderful.

Helen: My kids drive the janitors crazy.

Jack: I feel sorrier for us, I mean from what we're describing tonight, right now. We're saying we need somebody, bad.

Betty: Or wish somebody needed us.

Mary: What kind of feedback do you get from parents? What reaction do you get from parents, mixed?

Will: Yes, they get pretty damn frustrated because gee, the kid has been in there six months. I thought he was going to go to college next year!

Mary: I had a letter like that. I've gone along with all the testing, I've gone along with all the program, and nothing seems to be helping. What's the problem?

Thus, all group members are experiencing intense loneliness and alienation from a wide diversity of sources. But note that this is a group-wide experience. Small group research has consistently demonstrated that threat or commonly perceived hostility directed broadly toward members of a group will significantly increase the level of cohesiveness within that group. (Blake & Mouton, 1961; Myers, 1962; Pepitone & Kleiner, 1957; Sherif & Sherif, 1963; Wilson & Miller, 1961) This cohesiveness-enhancement by group-wide threat is precisely what occurred within our teacher group. For example, after the several discussions of loneliness noted above, the following interaction took place:

Jack: You're describing, to say the least, this has been a very different kind of group meeting.

Barbara: What I felt was everybody was, you know, somebody would say something and all of a sudden somebody else would jump in and say the same point.

Will: It seemed awful easy to express your feelings.

Barbara: We were all jumping in the same pond, and you know, it was comfortable sinking. Now we need artificial respiration.

Mary: But we're alone together now.

Just as the augmenting of cohesiveness appeared to be a consequent of the group's shared perception of aloneness and threat, cohesiveness too had its consequences. In the few minutes remaining in this session after the excerpt noted above, the group reached its greatest depth of openness yet experienced in a discussion of intense hostility toward certain pupils. This enhanced level of openness continued to be repeatedly apparent in the group meetings which followed.

Session 10.   Agreeing to Disagree

Helen opened this session by re-presenting the pupil she had discussed in the fourth session. As was true for all group member re-presentations, however, the emphasis this time was clearly and openly upon her feelings and her stake in the teacher-pupil relationship. It will be recalled that when Helen first presented this pupil during the fourth session, a great deal of rapid fire and at times somewhat hostile questioning of her ensued. Perhaps we learn something about Helen, and the possibility that she is easy prey in this group, from the fact that, in this tenth session also, a good deal of negative questioning and disagreement emerged. *However*, most important to note here is the changed quality of the disagreement as a function of what clearly seems to be the corresponding change in group trust and comfort. In the fourth session a peer court emerged, Helen was grilled and all members were clearly uncomfortable. By this tenth session, however, openness was consistently the group's norm, intermember attraction was high and, as others (Frank, 1957; Goldstein, Heller & Sechrest, 1966) have observed occurs when a group is highly cohesive, the members with relative comfort began to agree to disagree.

We have noted in earlier sessions that there existed a marked contrast in Jack's and Will's leadership behavior. One dimension of this contrast was the frequent manner in which Will slid into the role of group member, exploring his feelings in a manner which apparently contributed little to the group's movement. Early in this tenth session, for example, the following interchange took place:

Helen: Yes, but don't you ever have doubts that what you're bringing out should be brought out? I think that's what I was feeling.

Will: I think you did too. That's what I remember about it and remember sharing the anxiety with you. . .

Barbara: That's why I say you bring out this behavior and how do you handle it. Suddenly you think, my God, I've worked this far for this? You know, look what I'm doing!

Will: Yes, my immediate response to this is that you bring me for example a hell of a lot of relief when you tell me that this kid looks that way he does now and everything because you were so anxious about it you made me feel very anxious about it.

Helen: I was very anxious about it, but I'm not anymore. I probably would be if he was the same, but he's moved on.

Will: Yes, that's right, I mean that's why I feel like thank heavens, like you've really kind of set us at ease. . .

Similarly, the following occurred late in the session:

Will: No, but the fact is the kid is helping himself.
Ken: Yes.
Will: And I was giving him no credit.
Ken: I thought you said. . .
Will: I needed the credit more than the kid.
Betty: Especially . . . if we believe in the idea that you can help the child become what he wants to become. Now he has the power to do that.
Will: Right.
Betty: Now who are we to, you know. . .
Will: So what the hell are we doing then?
Jack: Oh, we're talking about we're getting the kicks.
Will: Right, exactly.
Ken: Shouldn't we take any credit? I'm asking that you almost seem, you know, uncomfortable that you did.
Will: Well, let's put it this way. I think I have a right to take some credit in what happened to that kid.
Ken: Okay.
Will: There's no question about that, but I think after this period of time I'm taking too much of the credit. That's what I think is bothering me.

Will's comments again stand in marked contrast to Jack's approach to the group. The following excerpts, all involving Jack, and from different points in this session, demonstrate in a variety of ways the manner in which Jack succeeded in consistently letting the group's needs determine his behavior.

1. Restructuring toward a teacher focus.

Jack: Well, that's it. I think we've put our finger on the feeling and the concerns when we convey something to a youngster like, Okay Johnny, we've worked like beavers all year and are you going to let it crumble around you? I think that says an awful lot about us . . . Is that a message for Johnny or is it, as we are saying, what are you about to do to all of my laboring? We've built this little schema all year and it's going to crumble. It seems to me there is more of us in that kind of communication than there is of Johnny, or it's at least as relevant for us as it is for him.

2. *Reflection of feeling.*

Betty: I almost wish we had a tyrannical leader to say we're going to talk about this . . . I feel we're so flakey, we're all over the place.

Helen: Yes.

Ken: Yes, I feel the same way.

Betty: But why are we so flakey?

Jack: You think it would be easier if somebody made these decisions, rather than you?

3. *Interpretation.*

Jack: It's interesting that in all of our other sessions we've talked about how sick the kids are, and how bad off things are. Now tonight for the first time we latched on to the possibility that some of the youngsters are in fact better. That things are not as bad as they were and I'm wondering if this is more difficult for us to talk about. That maybe we thrive on pathology. . .

Betty: You mean we need them to be sick?

4. *Cohesiveness augmentation.*

Jack: You know the other thing I can't help but feel that has happened tonight is that for the first time when somebody makes a statement or gives an interpretation, that there isn't some kind of wholesale acceptance (of it). As I think back on the other meetings we've had, if somebody does give a little of themselves typically . . . people have kind of popped on the wagon and said "me too." Tonight, though, it doesn't seem to be happening that way. People have disagreed, they've challenged, they've stuck to their own interpretations.

Thus the group leaders continued to behave in accord with their very different leadership styles, styles whose differences we have gone to some lengths to highlight since a modified group-centered approach seems to have contributed so much to the group's movement, and a directive approach so little.

Also noteworthy about this session was the manner in which all group members discussed at length the ambivalence they experience when a pupil "graduates" from their class to a regular class. They are pleased but also vaguely discomforted by the separation involved. Several members clearly identified very strongly with given pupils, so much so that their unwillingness to "give up" the pupil was quite strong. Ken captured this reluctance to "let go" well with his comment. . . . He was going back to a regular class. "If you've ever built something, especially an airplane, if you fly it it's liable to smash completely apart and there's a terrible reluctance to let it go on its own." Statements such as these are also of interest beyond their specific content as they illustrate the manner in which Ken, the group's most resistive member until recent sessions, had increasingly "joined the group" in his willingness to openly examine and share his own feelings nondefensively.

Session 11.   The Depth of Feeling

This session was unequivocally the group's best to this point. Very little resistiveness was present; both group leaders were consistently empathic; Ken continued to display movement, closing further the gap between himself and the rest of the group; and most noteworthy, for the group as a whole the level of openness displayed involved greater intouchness with self and greater depth of feeling than had been true in any other session.

Pat opened the session by re-presenting, with much greater focus upon her own feelings, the pupil she had discussed at an earlier meeting.

Pat: I was able to have him stay after school and then take him home and, oh, it was really terrible. I took him home and there is this area where all the rivers are and the houses or shacks . . . there are eleven people in Roger's family and his house was down this dirt, muddy road with all kinds of ruts and water. A two room house, unpainted . . . I had a physical reaction, kind of sick, it was really terrible . . . I really don't see where this child exists and I think what it really made me wonder is what can you really do about the kids. If you were driving along and you saw an unpainted board building you would think now somebody keeps their tools in there. But people really lived in it, and I'm really hung up on that. I had to get out of the house after I got home because I didn't want to think about it. How much can you really feel you know what he's feeling? How can you really know about what his life is like?

Jack: So it raises concerns that you have, not only about Roger, but about yourself.

Pat: Yes, how much can you really understand. . . What can I do for this kid when he is in a place like this. . . There are some things you can do but it seems like the odds are so overwhelming.

Jack: This sounds like it was quite an emotional experience for you today, Pat.

Pat: It really was. I was driving back. This other girl who teaches with me . . . we didn't speak for a real long time. I was really sick to my stomach and I had tears in my eyes and I just thought, oh, you know, what can you do?

*   *   *

Barbara: Sometimes it makes you feel like a number one heel when they come in and they're dirty. . .

Jack: Pardon?

Pat: That used to bother me a lot last June.

Barbara: And you know, you think you can go to one of these discount places and buy him a new pair of shoes. It at least would be something for them. You know, to me I think it sometimes makes you feel terribly, terribly selfish. It does me anyway . . . I'm with Pat, it hurts.

*   *   *

Mary: What she mentioned raised a question of guilt which I think maybe we could go into a little bit more. Yesterday and today I've been feeling extremely guilty about something. I thought it might be a good thing to talk about, that is how much guilt do we feel for them as teachers of these kids when we make decisions and everything goes haywire. Just how much responsibility do we have? What do we do about the guilt feelings. Can we function after something has happened that we feel so guilty about? Well, for example, one of the boys that entered my class in September. . . Well, he has been under a psychologist's care for over a year and he was a very disturbed boy, but during the summer he had made tremendous progress according to the psychologist and the first couple of days in class I saw he was a boy who was working out his problems quite well. Then he started reacting against the class and he was falling to pieces. My immediate reaction was to take him out of the class and put him in a regular class. So I just went ahead and suggested this and the psychologist backed it up completely. But I was the one who first suggested it. He was all right for quite a while and all of a sudden— *boom*. He started down, they moved and he went to one of the city schools. He tried to hang himself. When I heard this, boy, I don't know, how can we continue to work. Like I've got a boy right now and I don't think he should come back next year and I'm afraid to say it. I'm terrified.

These excerpts in many senses speak for themselves. They stand in very marked contrast to the superficiality, self-avoidance and pupil-centeredness of earlier sessions, and mark well the progress the group members have made to this point.

Session 12.   A Beginning Look Outside

The very deep level of openness characteristic of the previous meeting continued during this session, as did complimentary feelings of trust and group cohesiveness. There existed during this session a growing focus upon the "here and now" flow of interpersonal traffic within the group, i.e., a more direct and personalized examination of how the members were perceiving and effecting one another. Perhaps most significant of this session, however, was the manner in which the group began to edge toward its third and final phase. In the introduction to this chapter we depicted three phases or a basic progression in this group's functioning. The Pupil-Centered and Teacher-Pupil Relationship Centered phases have been amply documented in our session by session analysis to this point. During this twelfth session the group members, acknowledging the very fundamental and open manner in which feelings were being looked at, began to ask the question: What next? How, they began to explore, could the in-touchness and authenticity being experienced be put to constructive use in their classroom situations? Thus the members began to enter the New Problem Solving phase of the group's development.

In describing the openness characteristic of the group's interactions in recent sessions, we indicated that such openness about self during "case" re-presentation stood in marked contrast to that during the original presentation of the "problem pupil." On page 75 to concretely illustrate this change, is an excerpt from Barbara's sixth session presentation of her problems with John. Note the manner in which all of her diverse feelings expressed in this excerpt were covered up, tangentially revealed or simply latent and knowable to us only by inference. Contrastingly, we see quite a different pattern of openness and nondefensiveness in the following excerpt from her re-presentation of this pupil:

> I related last time . . . that they definitely felt he was eventually homicidal or suicidal . . . I don't know, I guess he does leave me kind of powerless. You want to help him and yet you know there is so much there . . . I thought I'd seen every behavior going that would make me come up with feelings of repulsion. . . . I didn't think I could see anything that would take me back like this particular one did. They were out there and the one boy was sitting up in his chair. I guess he had his head down on the floor and he gassed and John just rammed his face in his fanny and started smelling. It really showed to me how really sick John was . . . it never has bothered me but when I saw this it took everything it could not to really just

lay him out. . . It really was repulsive to me and it took me with John I think a couple of days at least not to think back. . . And since then working with him is frustration to me in many ways. . . The other thing that's hard with working with John is the way he manipulates the whole group. . . The more I've seen it the more I can see where some of my anger is probably coming through.

*   *   *

I think a part of what I felt was I did feel sorry for this kid because he gets so little out of life, so very little. And I guess no matter which way I handled him I felt guilty about it. . . I didn't want to show anger and yet I was angry.

As happens characteristically in highly cohesive groups, openness begets openness and thus, Barbara's statements led to similar explorations of their own feelings of powerlessness, compassion and anger by Helen, Mary and Ken.

We indicated above that the group evidenced beginning steps into their New Problem Solving phase. During their earlier Pupil-Centered phase, pupil management *without* reference to teacher feelings was the focus. Now, with teacher feelings and relationship concerns openly being examined, such emphases were heavily drawn upon as the group in a sense began to return to the classroom and to view pupil management in a much more meaningful and potentially much more helpful manner. Note, for example, the balanced view of pupil *and* teacher contributions to classroom events evident in the following excerpt:

Ken: I'll tell him it's all right, you're not going to be punished for it but in the long run I wish you wouldn't do that. Not the first day but sooner or later I have to tell him that some of the reaction he's getting is me. That I can't stand that and it really bothers me. In fact one of the kids can babble and babble and I just look at him and say will you please stop.

Mary: Well, they just have to read it on my face. Like yesterday . . . they knew it and they told me and they gave it to me all day.

Ken: If they read it and you won't admit it, and if they read it in me and I won't admit it, I'm in trouble.

Jack: Aren't we really saying we've got all these feelings and they are obviously potent, and what do we do with them?

New Problem Solving, from a joint teacher-pupil perspective, continued to develop more fully as the remaining sessions unfolded.

Session 13.   The Leaders Clash

As a group develops trust, openness, a measure of self-direction and modes of interacting which it finds relatively comfortable, there emerges correspondingly less need for formal leadership. This was indeed the case during the last few sessions immediately preceding this one and, as the reader has noted, we have had relatively little to say about Jack and Will for these last few sessions. The leaders, one might suppose, were intentionally and appropriately less active serving as occasional catalysts, stimulants or moderators as the group successfully explored its deeper feelings. Furthermore, one might speculate that the group's behavior would serve to maintain or reinforce for the leaders the appropriateness of their own behavior. Such indeed seems to have been the case for Jack, who, during this session, behaved in ways clearly consistent with his earlier behavior. Will, however, did not. It is likely that he failed to appreciate the manner in which even highly open groups move in waves, with occasional and perhaps necessary periods of superficiality emerging among the long stretches of revelation and exploration. He seemed during this session to be, in a sense, impatient of any member superficiality and on several occasions sought to actively direct a member into openness. We have commented earlier on the ways in which such direct persuasive efforts are almost always destined to fail, and such was indeed the case here. His forceful exhortations combined with his member-like personalizing also noted earlier to clearly detour the group's efforts for most of this session. The following excerpts are representative of the exhortational and personalizing detour signs which Will erected during this session:

Will: What we did last week, really talk to each other, I thought it was very hard to do.

Jack: You're talking now about when we started talking about our feelings about. . .

Will: Right, not at the end . . . one of the feelings that I have is almost a kind of disappointment in us that we aren't able to just kind of keep going at the same level that we had gotten to last week.

             *   *   *

Betty: Working in Balton for a year with five year olds . . . one week when I wasn't supposed to be there I was walking down the street and I saw one of them. Well, hello, Kevin (I said). He walked right by as though he didn't know me.

Ken: Right.

Betty: My God!
Jack: Remember me, I'm the one who loves you.
Will: Right. I had the same damn experience. It was at Balton.
           I had this group of little five year olds and that kid . . . I
           let them beat me up in games all year . . . I had ulcers
           over that damn kid and when I started telling him about,
           you know, June was coming and this good little social worker
           was going to be leaving and then he really beat me up and
           all this. As you know, I came back a couple of months
           later and the kid hardly remembered my name. I really could
           have smashed him right in the mouth. It was one thing for
           him to separate, but did he have to do it so completely?
           Is that all I meant to him? Obviously he meant more to me
           than I meant to him.

                    *   *   *

Jack: Ken, I think I really got close to it just now when he said
           if you use emotionally charged statements and you can't
           predict how the other person is going to react. I think that's
           exactly what we're trying to solve now, are we engaging in
           risk taking kinds of behaviors? Can we say something and
           still feel like we can come back next week?
Will: Yes, can you say to Mary, you know, shut up for a minute
           will you. I'm not through, I'm right in the middle of this
           and I'm not getting any reactions and I don't know if I like
           your reaction right now!
Ken: I don't know. I can know the person and respond that way.
           But if they don't know me they are not going to accept
           my response for what it is until we get to that level.
Will: How the hell do you get to that level?
Ken: Oh, we're getting there.
Will: Not by doing it the way you're doing it.
Ken: Sure you will.
Will: I don't agree. I think that you would have gotten to know
           her a hell of a lot more if you had said that, because
           then she could have said something to you and then you
           could have understood each other. And then everything
           would have been in its place.

                    *   *   *

Will: We challenged this last week and we said, yes, it's okay
           to do this. It's okay to move in and to express. And what I'm
           saying is that by you or anyone else in this group not
           taking a chance you're hurting the purpose of this group and
           the rest of us can't allow it.

This type of effort by Will led Jack to more and more directly
challenge him, commenting that openness can't be "legislated" and,

finally, in a direct confrontation, Jack asked Will: "Aside from our brow beating of Ken, maybe the question that Ken's asking is have we created the kind of climate where we are safe and comfortable?" Will missed the referrant of this question totally, for his response was: "Yes, Jack, that's what I was trying to say. I feel that it is an obligation of all of us in the group that if we see a person seeking such safety by not expressing, it's an obligation the rest of us have to draw it out."

This session, however, was not totally lacking in group movement. Ken re-presented and teacher-pupil separation was his major theme. Jack, Betty and Ken elaborated this theme and it was clear that end-of-term separation presented a major emotional problem not only for the pupils, but for the teachers also. Furthermore, there were hints at times that the focus on separation and loss also was the group's way of beginning to deal with its own termination a few sessions hence.

Session 14.   Alone, Alone, Alone

Two major themes dominated this fourteenth session. The group returned, in forces as it were, to examine the sense of aloneness they had explored several times before. Such feelings were expressed in this session much more deeply and broadly than had been true in the past. Secondly, the detours of the last session seemed overcome, and the group entered more fully into their New Problem Solving phase with several discussions of the implications of lessons learned within the group for out-group living.

Betty re-presented and quite rapidly launched upon the loneliness theme, commenting for example that "you're really alone in the kinds of decisions you have to make," "nobody else really knows what it's like to live in the (class) room," and "there's nobody else around who can lead the kid's behavior any better than you can and that's the kind of loneliness that eats at you." The theme spread rapidly. Several members similarly decried the unsplendid isolation within which they worked. Ken pointed to alienation from pupils' parents, Barbara re-raised difficulties with and distance from regular teachers, Pat agreed and elaborated Barbara's feelings, Helen spoke of separateness from others on the school payroll, and so forth. However, in contrast to earlier group-wide discussions of aloneness—in which there was agreement but little constructive growth from sharing—the group was now in a much better position to meaningfully use their shared feelings and perceptions. Most of this usage took form in generalizing and re-examining from past feelings to current dilemmas outside the group. For example, in the following excerpt Jack helped the group perceive the elements common to both the teacher and pupil sense of aloneness. Teacher understanding of both pupil and self was thus augmented.

Jack: Isn't the exciting thing about what we're saying now that the kids and the teachers have feelings that are almost identical? I mean we're feeling thwarted, not being responded to, lack of feedback, or we're in a world of our own.

Betty: This is exactly what happens. I thought of this the other day. Once in a class at SU, some teacher, I think it was you. . . One of the very first classes I took. . . Teachers become like the kids they work with. Teachers become classified as the kids do.

Jack actively pursued this notion, and below, more directly urged the group to use their understanding of in-group interactions to clarify out-group events.

Jack: What we kind of started to do tonight was to relate how some of our feelings are almost identical to the feelings that the kids have. I'm wondering . . . would it be worth our time in the groups spending the sessions that we have been talking about our behavior in the group—what we've been saying, how we've been handling ourselves, how we feel and react—and drawing some comparisons with what we do with youngsters . . . I'm wondering if we aren't closer to spending our time this way. I don't know if we could have before . . . but it seems as if we're really headed that way. . . What made me focus on this was when we started talking about our ending the session, Ken made it very clear that the whole issue of separation was not something we were just talking about here, but (also) something he was involved in with his youngsters . . . I guess what I'm saying is that this may be the real world. That it's not just that we come together Wednesday nights and when we leave we pull the curtain. That what happens here, happens outside.

The group was clearly ready for this suggestion and, in fact, had been acting on it already but hadn't labeled it as such. Betty was first to respond to Jack's invitation:

Betty: The way I relate to what was just said in regard to does our participation in this group somehow reflect our participation in the classroom. Certainly there are many ways. The first one that comes to mind is when that guy . . . well

I do this often in school. I let people know things, sometimes it's very direct and very clear. I just have to let them
know. Not that I call them names or anything but, boy,
if it comes out, that's the way it is . . . for example, this
is when a kid should be in regular class. They should be
there for three weeks and poor teaching is going on and
moves aren't being made . . . so finally at one staff meeting,
when somebody is still tip-toeing around, I will make a
statement like—which is certainly not nice and not courteous
—after February first that child will not be allowed in my
room! You know, the point is made, there is no more
discussion, it's understood but it's not very nice. Well,
that certainly has happened here.

      *   *   *

Another thing is when I turned to Barbara two weeks ago
and said something about feeling tone. I have never talked
feeling tone to any other adult until that night but I felt it
time and time again in school. What the hell, don't talk
as though you're concerned about the kid when you sound
like you're on the golf course.

Others responded similarly as the session progressed:

Jack: Just to trace what I think has happened. We started with
spending X amount of time on the youngsters. Then we
started talking about ourselves, kind of as individuals. And
more recently I think we started to talk about ourselves
more as a group and what happens here and how we handle
ourselves and react to each other. Now I guess Betty is saying and I'm saying and Will and perhaps a few others, can
we make analogies, Barbara, of our behavior here in the
group to what happens in our contacts with people at school.

Pat: There's lots of parallels. I think in this group sometimes
I'm being quiet and then all of a sudden I'll say something.
And other times I kind of jerk around. That's just the way
I am with those kids. I'll go along and be calm and quiet
and all of a sudden, oh, what kind of class is this!

      *   *   *

Ken: If we relate to each other in certain way here, this is how
we relate in the classroom. There are parallels in the
classroom. This group, being here, changes the way we relate.
And the classroom changes it too. . . If we have a certain
pattern of interaction with people and it's here in the group,
and it's roughly similar or very similar with the kids and
you can see tremendous changes here in fourteen weeks,
I wonder what the group has done to me since September.

They are people and they are more intensely people because
. . . your relations are much much stronger or I wouldn't
be worrying about kids going up and down the steps.

*　　　　　　　*　　　　　　　*

Mary: We had a meeting last week . . . and a science teacher was
saying how when report cards come out you put the grades
on the board and he says, you who receive this grade are
in the top quarter. You are at the bottom quarter if you
receive this grade and, being used to this group, I yelled
out "pressure."

And, perhaps augmenting the adage that those who teach, learn in
the process and those who provide psychotherapy gain self-insights
in the process we find the following group leader statement:

Will: I know that I have a tendency to dominate a group and
talk too much in it. I think I've worked on myself in this
group as a result of some of the reactions that I've seen
and that I've felt and I think this helps me. I think it's
helped me to shut my mouth a few times this year when
it's been very helpful, when it wouldn't have accomplished
anything.

Jack: It's done the opposite for me in a number of situations.
I'm involved in a number of situations where I'm expected
to be the objective participant, bystander, and there have
been lots of times here when I don't feel so objective
and one of the things that has made me feel good is that
I don't have to feel that objective. . . So I find myself
contrasting what happens here and what happens in other
situations.

Session 15.　　From In-Group to Out-Group and Back

At an ever-increasing rate, and with ever greater depth and meaning-
fulness, the group resumed its problem solving exploration of the
relationships between in-group and out-group interactions. The interactions at the very opening of the session, and in unbroken form well
into the session, illustrate the growing facileness of the group in this
in-group to out-group and back regard:

Jack: Last week we began to focus on how we've been spending
our time here as a group and trying to see some ways that
our behavior and our reactions here seem to have some correlations with children and with adults outside of their
meetings. I think that's about where we ended.

Helen: After the meeting last Wednesday . . . the next day I had

	a well, what would you call it, an evaluation with my principal and supervisor. I was amazed . . . because I was always using the same words or technique and it was very funny, I was working in the same way I was working, we were working in the group.
Jack:	Could you give some example?
Helen:	Like when all of a sudden maybe one member was really putting it on the other person, where a response had to be made . . . and so many times I caught them off guard because I sit there and say all right, and this one time I don't respond and it got them all shook up . . . I think one of the main things is . . . what this group has done by hearing many things, and knowing, in some respects I'm not alone . . . and in other respects that it's okay that I'm working in this way. This gave me the confidence I needed that I don't think I would have had previously. . . We're at the point at these meetings where we aim for communication and understanding so it's not just verbal back and forth. . . What often happens when you're talking to somebody, especially in a meeting like that, is terminology is going back and forth but the clarification and communication isn't there. And working in this group I was able to stop and ask for clarification and working feelings in . . . I was sensitive. It gave me strength when I needed strength.
Will:	In other words you felt, kind of, a little more sure of yourself.
Helen:	It's not as simple as that. I can't say just what it was. . . It's been the way we have learned to work in a group and you can't just say that it's assuredness. I have to use at least six different adjectives, a greater awareness of myself, better understanding of their predicament. . . Trying it in and pulling in so well . . . what I saw the need for where as I wouldn't have bothered before. And just many skills. I'm talking about skills but there were many feelings involved too.

*   *   *

	They (principal and supervisor) were questioning my whole philosophy of working with children. If we bring visitors into your room and you don't look like a good teacher, the classroom doesn't look like a good class, and this is what you have to attain. You have to present an image, and children have to present an image. And I looked at him, back to him and I said you're sure this is what you want to say?
Ken:	You were loaded for bear.
Helen:	What they were saying is that feelings shouldn't be dealt with and they should learn to park them at the door.
Mary:	Well, why don't they do away with the program, why

bother? You might as well have a straight teacher in front of the room.

Helen: Well, they said to me . . . they said we feel there have to be certain changes for what we want in the program. We don't want you to feel too uncomfortable. I said, all right you can stop right there. You have my answer, I won't be here next year. I believe in the way I work and the philosophy I have. . . If this is what you have and this is the way you perceive the program to be and you believe in it, look for a different person. . . So the next hour and a half was building Helen up.

Barbara: Telling her to change?

Helen: No, oh no. Building her up and building her up and changing some of the statements or trying to iron out some of the statements that had been made.

Ken: What for?

Helen: What for? They refused to take my resignation . . . I was then called in after school was out by the administrator of the building who seemed very anxious. Wanted to know why I thought, why I reacted, and then I named off ten criticisms in every area. And he said, no, no, I don't want you to feel like this. He said I like you so much as a person and I said I don't care, don't like me as a person, I said I want you to like me as a teacher, you know, respect me as a teacher. I don't care what you think of me as a person, which he couldn't react to, and I got it from this meeting because we were talking about exactly that thing and how it affected us.

This interaction continued further in the direction of attempts at new problem solving:

Jack: Do you think there's any analogy between your principal saying I like you as a person but don't like the way you teach and what we say to youngsters.

Helen: Yes, or you know when we send a child home and the next day it's very important to know they know that we haven't rejected them. We are very friendly toward the child; and that's the way I felt was happening at the meeting, you know, after school. He had to reinforce, exactly what we do for the child.

Pat: What if something like that were pointed out . . . to the supervisor. You know, what you're doing to me now is one of the things I try to do to children, with children. What kind of a reaction would we have? . . . Point out to them that there are parallels between how you react and act with children and how they react and act with you and whether that might be some bridge of understanding.

These excerpts represented member growth to which both group leaders responded with immediate reward:

Jack: I think one of the dynamic things about what you've described is that one of the ways you acted, or lots of the ways you acted, did in fact change the behavior of the other people, really in a more positive direction even though you saw it as kind of hypocritical, first rejection then patting you on the back. But on the other hand, they apparently on some level were genuinely concerned.

Helen: Yes.

Will: It sounds like you have a feeling about what it was all about and what was going on and instead of being a recipient of their criticism, because you were aware of what was going on, you could question them. And I think because you were aware of your own feelings and what they were talking about you just weren't defensive.

Helen: The realization that you didn't have to always answer, you could ask the questions back.

These attempts at problem solving combined with the leader's explicit approval to produce two significant and positive consequents during this session. First, additional in-group, out-group comparisons emerged and were used by Betty and Barbara in further attempts at constructively dealing with classroom problem situations. Secondly, in a complementary manner, group cohesiveness was clearly augmented and loneliness reduced. Thus there emerged statements such as Barbara's:

> Every time someone (in the group) spoke I felt like it was me. . . Suddenly there are eight people in the room and yet it's all you. . . We talked about loneliness last week and . . . through hearing others and knowing that you're not alone in this has ridded me of some of my loneliness . . . I feel like I'm a part of something much bigger than just myself out there fighting the battle . . . I've taken something from everybody in the group and . . . to me this has been . . . my strength because I'm not just learning more and more . . but now I'm kind of eight.

In all, this fifteenth session was unusually productive and cohesiveness-enhancing.

Session 16.   Problem Solving and Resolution of Resistance

The group's attempts to draw constructive out-group lessons from in-group interactions continued at a high level during this session. The increasing personalization and depth of these attempts not surprisingly elicited new dimensions of member resistance, which the group was largely able to resolve. The re-emergence of member resistance, however, should serve to illustratively underscore that such a phenomenon is always potentially present even when a group has reached very high levels of openness in its interactions.

The constructive lessons drawn during the session were varied. Pat described, as Helen had in the previous session, how a difficult interaction with her principal was handled differently and more adequately by her by applying insights gleaned from within-group interactions. Betty, with Jack's assistance, drew meaningful parallels between end of term feelings experienced by her pupils and end of group feelings currently operating within the teacher group. Ken, again with help from Jack, became more able to see the relatedness of his not infrequent closedness and need for control in his classroom and analogous behaviors within the group. Here, as in the examples above, the group appropriately focused upon not only classroom-group similarities but also realistic discriminations between the two. The dimensions of responsibility and authenticity in class and within the group were contrasted and compared by several group members. Pat and Ken discussed at some length differences and similarities between the group meetings and their conception of group psychotherapy, a discussion which Jack extended to include the issue of within-group versus within-class teacher exposure of self. Finally, and by way of transition to the issue of within-group resistance, Betty, Barbara, and Pat, in an emotionally loaded interchange, examined their handling of anger directed at them by their pupils and anger directed at them within the group.

A group's progression toward openness, as has been illustrated in a number of earlier sessions, proceeds in waves. In beginning meetings, the troughs of resistance were long and frequent, the peaks of openness short and rare. By this sixteenth session the opposite circumstance prevailed. The substance of the group's openness, however, revolved around highly personal and rather charged topics, i.e., authenticity, anger, defensiveness, exposure, etc. The substance of the resistance engendered by this intense openness, while clearly revealed, differed in nature from the flight to superficiality and intellectualization characteristic of early session resistance. It took form largely in within-group hostility and open disclaimers that *this* group was not a psychotherapy group, and hence the discussion of certain topics was inappropriate.

Not only are the forms resistance takes early and late in a group's life different but, correspondingly, the most appropriate means of resolving such resistance differ. As will be recalled, early resistance in this group had to be and was dealt with slowly and indirectly, with the leaders encouraging the members toward openness very gradually concomitant with the all important development of within-group trust—the pace of which was largely determined by the group members. By this stage in the group's life, trust had developed to high levels, members were well practiced in openness and, thus, the need for slowness and indirection in seeking to reduce resistances had largely diminished. The leaders were aware of this greater freedom for frontally attacking resistances, a procedure which they used with a fair degree of success, as the following excerpts illustrate. The first interaction below represents an attempt by Jack to teach Ken that his and the group's continued reluctance to challenge Jack is unnecessary and, more generally, that authority figures *can* be challenged even within the group:

Jack: Ken, you're smiling but I think you're angry. Are you?
Ken: No, I'm not angry, but. . .
Betty: A little upset?
Ken: A little upset maybe, yes.
Jack: Who are you upset at?
Ken: Well, I'd be upset at the person who posed the question.
Jack: Who was the person that posed the question . . . it was me.
Ken: Okay, but, okay, you were the last one that said it.
Jack: Yes, I've felt very left out because a lot of people have come in for some of their lumps and nobody has ever challenged anything I've ever said. In a couple of instances you have been the one who has been accused of changing the course of conversation, haven't you? And I've personally been the one who has said that to you.
Ken: Well, I guess. . .
Jack: I think I hooked on that because of my earlier comment that there do seem to be some things that are on, you know, a lot of our minds about what's happening in the group that we don't seem to be talking about.

Not only does Jack's offering of "permission to challenge" here help Ken do so, but it serves as a model to the rest of the group, communicating, in a sense, the appropriateness of their behaving similarily. Thus, in the excerpt below, Barbara is able (with the help of yet further "permission" or encouragement from Jack) to speak openly about hostility she feels toward Betty which originated in the previous session.

Jack: I think that I agree. I think that there has been a great reluctance on all of our parts to disagree or to turn to somebody and say, I think that's a lot of baloney. Maybe there are other ways to do it . . . and I think we've found them all. And a lot of them haven't been very satisfactory (but) we continued to do it that way. So when something happened last week that was much more open and to the point. . .

Barbara: Yes, I thought we were dealing with feelings, Betty and I. She had one, I had another. We weren't communicating. When you don't communicate I think it brings out certain anger in us because we want to communicate with people . . . I'm not going to never speak to Betty again simply because we didn't agree on one point and one meeting. I didn't feel that . . . I didn't mean for the rest of the time I wasn't going to talk to Betty.

*   *   *

Barbara: I had a great deal of doubt as to where angry feelings lead us and a great deal of feeling that anger feelings are only negative. We'll never be friends, you can't communicate. All right, we've expressed it, now where are we going to go from here . . . I don't think that ever came out, that angry feelings can be resolved in the group and it can go on. . .

And thus the group was ever-more able to deal effectively and non-resistively with themselves and their interpersonal impacts both within and outside the group.

Session 17.   Finale . . . Almost

This was to be the group's last meeting. Early in its progress the group members suggested and agreed to have a social meeting, or, in a sense, "going away party" the next week. Thus, the "final" meeting to be discussed below was the group's last "business" meeting. Its substance was quite similar to those sessions immediately preceding it, i.e. marked openness and numerous attempts, most of them successful, to draw upon and learn from in-group and out-group similarities and differences.

Betty and Barbara opened the session by sharing with the group the ways in which they were able to not only resolve their conflict of two weeks ago, but also the ways in which the two of them have grown closer for having done so. Mary, Helen and Barbara seized upon this interaction to draw direct implications for the handling of teacher-directed pupil anger in the classroom. Of interest here is not only that they did so, but did so with little urging or direction from the group leaders, thus perhaps demonstrating beginning success by the group members at what may be the group's most important goal—augmenting the degree to which the members are armed after the group dissolves with more effective modes of classroom-relevant problem solving techniques. As this theme developed, its discussion was joined by Ken and Pat who not only elaborated the in-group to out-group notions indicated above, but generalized such notions to the impact within-group and within-class of teacher anxiety. In the most basic senses, these types of member-originated and self-focusing successful attempts at new problem solving were the most complete affirmation to date that the group was functioning very close to the ideal manner originally aspired to by the group leaders. Several aspects of these dimensions are illustrated in the following excerpt:

Jack: So you're really saying that we tell the kids this all year, okay, you've got feelings, express them if you have to and we'll accept them and hopefully deal with them. But when we're involved with some of the same kinds of feelings we may not practice on ourselves what we are preaching to the kids. And even when it happened here in the group . . . it was kind of like, gee, too bad it happened sort of. In other words, we weren't able to use it, quote, therapeutically. I don't know, is this what you're saying?

Ken: You know, in September I wouldn't have been so angry, maybe I wouldn't let myself get angry. I figured I shouldn't. Now I figure sometimes I should get angry, real angry.

Betty: Yes, but look at the accumulation of anger . . . not just classroom or kids but of maybe everything around you kind of accumulates too, you know, gee, look what I'm doing and who knows it, who appreciates it, who? What's it all kind of adding up to anyway? Which is a question that comes along with fatigue . . . and I've been thinking . . . about the angry feelings inside and what do we do with them. The question is do you throw them back at the children? How do you throw them back, what do you do with them, and if you internalize them what does it do? It builds up and builds up and builds up. I hate to even enter the building, let alone see any of the adults in the building who don't know what you're doing. They represent some symbol toward which anger is directed, at least represent the conflict that you had to deal with all year long.

Jack: So then the way we handled ourselves a few weeks back around very strong feelings is close to the way that a lot of us are handling it now, with kids and adults.

There followed, during most of the remainder of this session, a series of similar interactions, in which varying group members indicated changes in out-group behavior growing from in-group events. Barbara drew analogies between unauthenticity or role playing in her classroom and during the earlier meetings of the teacher group. Mary described the positive effects which have followed from her increased forthrightness during a recent teacher conference at her school. Betty reported similar effects from changes in her conference behavior, changes she ascribed to lessons drawn from within-group interactions. Pat and Ken offered similar contributions.

SUMMARY

Our group dynamics examination of the seventeen teacher meetings is thus complete. Many aspects of these sessions have been discussed and illustrated, with primary attention devoted to three major themes— cohesiveness, phase movement and leadership. With regard to co-hesiveness, the flow of group events clearly demonstrated that, over sessions, resistiveness decreased to minimal levels along with compli-mentary increases in member attraction-to-group and self-disclosure. Clearly discernible phase movement in the group's interactions was also evident. From an early and almost exclusive pupil-centeredness, the group gradually moved toward a marked concern with teacher and teacher-pupil relationship dimensions of classroom living. This phase, in turn, combined with growing awareness within the group of its own interpersonal traffic to lead to the third and final phase of the group's functioning—new problem solving. Here, lessons learned about self and others within the group were constructively utilized by the mem-bers to plan and attempt new ways of relating and new problem solu-tions in their outside lives in general, and in their schools in particular.

Our session by session analysis also sought to highlight appropriate and inappropriate modes of group leadership. The consequences of varying leadership approaches within the group strongly confirm the appropriateness of an empathic, catalytic, moderately interpretive leader-ship style in which the message, "I understand and am with you," is consistently communicated to group members. Directiveness, exces-sive personalizing and full spontaneity, in contrast, appeared to yield negative effects, with member movement not resulting from these classes of leader behavior.

In a total sense, we view this group dynamics analysis as constituting a basic affirmation of the value of this approach for the goals we have set forth.

REFERENCES

Bach, G. R. *Intensive group psychotherapy* (New York: Ronald Press, 1954).

Bales, R. F. *Interaction process analysis: A method for the study of small groups* (Cambridge, Mass.: Addison-Wesley, 1950).

Bales, R. F., & Strodtbeck, P. L. Phases in group problem solving, *Journal of Abnormal Social Psychology*, 1951, **46**, 485–495.

Bion, W. R. *Experiences in groups* (New York: Basic Books, 1959).

Blake, R. R., & Mouton, J. S. Competition, communication and conformity. In I. A. Berg & B. M. Bass (Eds.) *Conformity and deviation* (New York: Harper, 1961), pp. 199–229.

Bradford, L. P., Gilob, J. R., & Benne, K. D. *T-group theory and laboratory method* (New York: Wiley, 1964).

Frank, J. D. Some determinants manifestations, and effects of cohesiveness in therapy groups, *International Journal of Group Psychotherapy*, 1957, 7, 53–63.

Goldstein, A. P., Heller, K., & Sechrest, L. B. *Psychotherapy and the psychology of behavior change* (New York: Wiley, 1966).

Golembiewski, R. T. *The small group* (Chicago: University of Chicago Press, 1962).

Gordon, T. *Group centered leadership* (Boston: Houghton Mifflin, 1955).

Heinicke, C., & Bales, R. F. Developmental trends in the structure of small groups, *Sociometry*, 1953, **16**, 20–34.

Hobbs, N. Group-centered psychotherapy. In C. R. Rogers (Ed.), *Client-centered therapy* (Boston, Houghton Mifflin, 1951), pp. 278–319.

Locke, N. M. *Group psychoanalysis* (New York: New York University Press, 1961).

Lowrey, L. G. Group therapy for mothers. *American Journal of Orthopsychiatry*, 1944, **14**, 589–592.

Martin, E., & Hill, W. F. A six phase theory of group development. *International Journal of Group Psychotherapy*, 1957, 7.

Myers, A. Team competition, success, and the adjustment of group members. *Journal of Abnormal Social Psychology*, 1962, **65**, 325–332.

Pepitone, A., & Kleiner, R. The effects of threat and frustration on group cohesiveness. *Journal of Abnormal Social Psychology*, 1957, **54**, 192–199.

Psathas, G. Phase movement and equilibrium tendencies in interaction process in psychotherapy groups, *Sociometry*, 1960, **23**, 177–194.

Schachter, S., Ellertson, N., McBride, D., & Gregory, D. An experimental study of cohesiveness and productivity. In D. Cartwright & A. Zander (Eds.), *Group dynamics* (Evanston, Ill.: Row, Peterson & Co., 1960), 150–160.

Sherif, M., & Sherif, C. W. *Groups in harmony and tension* (New York: Harper, 1953).

Truax, C. B., & Carkhuff, R. R. *Toward effective counseling and psychotherapy* (Chicago: Aldine, 1967).

Wilson, W., & Miller, N. Shifts in evaluations of participants following inter-group competition, *Journal of Abnormal Social Psychology*, 1961, **36**, 428–431.

Wolf, A., & Schwartz, E. K. *Psychoanalysis in groups* (New York: Grune & Stratton, 1962).

IV

To Be Or Not To Be: Dilemmas of Teachers in the Facilitation of Child Change

INTRODUCTION

Part III has attempted to highlight the interactions of our teacher group in a small group process experience over seventeen sessions. This group dynamics analysis provided many clues and insights into the complexities of teacher-child interactions. The present chapter will attempt to bring us even closer to the very personal concerns and perceptions that teachers of disturbed children have, particularly in one-to-one relationships.

In some ways it was not difficult at all to decide which themes should be given prominence in this chapter. One overriding concern expressed by the majority of our group had to do with their *realness* or authenticity for the children. How to be what you are as a human being and how to be what the children "need" became a central discussion. What if they, as teachers, didn't like themselves; thought of themselves as phonies; misperceived the needs of the children because they couldn't sort themselves out as persons? How connected is it necessary to become with children, or in other words, how far can and should a teacher go in establishing and maintaining relationships with children? Is it necessary for teachers to share secret parts of themselves with children, for them to engage in self-disclosure behaviors at the very same time they are encouraging children to do the same?

But what about the potentially devastating feedback from children who reflect the behaviors and attitudes that have been communicated to them by teachers? While paying lip service to the importance of attending to what children say to us and about us, it is quite another matter to be confronted with pieces of ourselves as portrayed by the children with whom we are involved.

We cannot lose sight of the fact that "love is not enough." There are behavioral incidents to understand and cope with; concepts and skills to be taught; and necessary communications to be effected between teachers and children and between teachers and other adults both in school and out. Then who is being asked to change? Can we request growth only on the part of the child? This group of teachers thought not. They recognized their interest, even obligation, to involve themselves in the change process. But how to do it!

Another theme discussed in this chapter is that of non-possessive presentation of self. As a condition for facilitating change in children, non-possessiveness was considered essential by many in the group. They found, however, that they came to identify so heavily with the children and their problems that they felt, and some even wanted, to intrude, to intervene, to place themselves between the child and the rest of the school environment. Certainly they recalled the lofty goal of providing the kind of environment in which children are aided in the internalization of their own controls and become self-directed. But somehow such cognitive awarenesses slip when a much involved teacher sees "her children" become the scapegoats for other school staff members who watch them like a hawk and pounce on them for the first infraction of table manners in the cafeteria.

Many in our group began to feel that the *empathic understanding* of what difficult children are experiencing is much more elusive than they were led to believe. The closer they grew to children in their rooms, the more seriously they questioned their ability to adequately step into the shoes of children and feel what they must be feeling. They felt uncomfortable, perhaps they couldn't assist children in their growth if there was such a gap in mutual understanding.

It may seem paradoxical to some readers that the theme of teacher *loneliness* is given such prominence in this book. To feel alone while surrounded by so many children, adults, behaviors and circumstances is not entirely comprehensible to those outside of the classroom. Interestingly enough, it was initially just as mystifying to this group of teachers. They could feel it more keenly than understand it. The realization that one is indeed lonely in the midst of one's day by day encounters with self, children and others is rather awesome and so it was for our group of teachers.

In reality, none of the above themes can stand alone. To highlight their separate importance, we have singled them out and given each of them some prominence. The reader will need to put them all back together into some mosaic that fits, at least for him. This is what the teachers tried to do. They grew to tolerate the ambiguity of not finding answers to their dilemmas, but acknowledged them and then turned to the strengths they had as helpers of children.

THE AUTHENTIC PRESENTATION OF SELF

Week after week, individual teachers talked about their lack of realization of who they were with children and what they were doing in their classrooms. Countless references always pivoted them back to an overwhelming feeling of insignificance as to the impact they were having on the children in their classes. Such references seemed to be in marked contrast to what the teachers were actually *doing* and more clearly reflected their feelings of impotence and growing cynicism. Wracked with self-doubts, they repeatedly verbalized judgmental statements about what they were and weren't doing. Such self-exploration led to the most basic relationship question of all; namely, how can one use oneself as a facilitator of children's learning and adjustment?

HOW DIFFICULT IT IS TO BE

The issue of using oneself as a change agent was reflected in an external concern with *doing something* and a less visible concern over *being* what you are. We sought with some success to get closer to ways in which one could represent oneself in an authentic manner and still *do something*. One of the more dramatic illustrations of this was in our discussions of physical contact with children.

> Barbara: . . . as I say, with John I love working with this kid, and yet you never feel like you're reaching him. At last I'm feeling something. I mean, he'll let me touch him. Now I can brush him on the head . . . I feel that he feels physically safe when you can bring him to you physically. Lately I have been able to put my arm around him, which is the first time since September. He just glues himself to you, like please protect me.

While some of the group members felt good about relating non-verbally and physically with children, for some it still presented some problems.

Mary: . . . I was sitting at the desk and finishing up some work before they came up and he came into the room, came up behind me trying to kiss me and maul me and all over me.

Barbara: How did you feel about that?

Mary: Awful, at that point terrible. . .

Ken also related a change in his behavior which addressed itself to the what-to-do question.

I don't know where it's from, but it's much different when I'm talking to a child. I spend half the time asking him or talking to him and all of a sudden I'm telling him how I feel. How I feel then and if I were in his position how I'd feel.

Very early in its meetings the group expressed the realization that while relationships with children must involve both the teacher and the child, the prevalent attitude in schools was that things are done *to* children by adults. We began by exploring the broad question of what it is that goes on when we talk about teachers and children relating together. What came up immediately was the difficult dichotomy of being coldly clinical versus humanly responsive.

Ken states in Session I:

It's not being unnatural, it's not going against yourself. It's just going against what a normal person could do—would do. . .

For any number of reasons, it seemed that many of them had dichotomized the "doing" to children as contrasted with "being" with children. They wondered if it would be enough to think and feel good things about children. Weren't there some "best" ways to go about interacting with difficult children? The tensions and pressures they felt seemed to propel them toward frameworks or handles which would allow them to concretize their interactions with the children.

Barbara: . . . teaching is action, there's no two ways about it. The more I think about the psychological aspects of working with the kids, you can have all the theories you want, but it's the on-the-spot strategic thing that really counts. When you're even talking about it after it happens, it's so much easier than being there and always saying the right thing at the right time under pressure. . .

What we began to see then, even in the first session, was vacillation between using one's own resources or utilizing a frame of reference to help one cope. Undergirding much of this discussion was the pressure to *do* something which would relieve a particular classroom problem. The pressure to act hastened our group's need and interest in looking at the children's responses to behaviors.

It was extremely difficult for our group to scrutinize their behaviors with children primarily because they had become aware of motivational forces within themselves that were both painful to look at and perhaps only partly conscious. They attempted to dig away at some interactions with children which reflected the dilemma of sorting their needs from those of children. As part of this project the children in each teacher's class were tested with a teacher-pupil relationship inventory. Ken related how one youngster balked and refused to even approach the room in which the testing was being done. He was encouraged by Ken to just go in and see what it was like. After much urging he did just that, but left quickly and as he passed the teacher he "gave me a big grin and said the trick didn't work. I went red, because I wasn't trying to trick him. And I didn't. I chewed him out really."

Helen asked: Why did you go red then?
Ken: Because I wasn't trying to trick him!
Betty: Just trying to what? To win?
Ken: Yes, I was trying to get him to fill that thing out, but not in a win-lose kind of thing. All of a sudden it became very important to me that he fill that out.

How quickly the youngster sensed that his needs were less at stake here than were those of the teacher. Subsequent dialogue between the group members revealed Ken's very angry feelings toward the child for not behaving as Ken felt he was able to: ". . . he is strong enough now that I don't see him as a child, that the handling has to be that special and that—oh, I don't know how to say it—gentle." Deeper and deeper the group scraped until it emerged that Ken had been grooming this boy as a potential group leader and *he*, the teacher, had been let down. But what the youngster was saying by his behavior, and words, was that he had enough problems and concerns of his own and he couldn't really help the teacher in arranging the group dynamics of the classroom.

This discussion led into a very lengthy debate over concepts of manipulation. We got stuck on terms like tricking, helping, manipulating, and so on. One of the themes we kept returning to was the discrepancy between our real intentions and what we actually do and say with children. The obvious complication is that such awareness is not always readily available, but that many members felt it was accessible if worked at. Earlier discussions of the need to do something came up again along with the group's own anger toward Ken at his behavior and unwillingness to look at it. At the very point in the group life when relationships were being discussed in terms of authenticity as a facilitating condition it was difficult for many group members to sort out what they were doing to Ken under the guise of helping him.

It was interesting to observe the gradual emergence of discussions which acknowledged the needs of teachers and how such need awareness influenced what is communicated to children. In many ways it sharpened many group members' ideas as to the meaning of being authentic and the effective use of self. One interchange which involved the clear setting of limits based on both what the child needed and what the teacher could tolerate was followed by a kind of post-mortem analysis which seemed meaningful to those participating:

Barbara: You're dealing with him as a real person.
Mary: Well, you're dealing with your own feelings.

*   *   *

Barbara: Sometimes it almost gets to be a cycle, you know, like you say, you feel guilty about it and I think you do. I think in dealing with these kids you feel like you've got to give every minute of every hour of every day.

We see, then, that at the core of the helping relationship is the giving of oneself; but our group continually asked how much should they and could they give. Self-awareness in and of itself was only seen by members of this group as a beginning step. What presented them with almost as much difficulty was what to do once they saw themselves more clearly. Seeing themselves more clearly was accomplished in many instances by teachers seeing themselves through a child's eyes. This section has attempted to highlight some of the interpersonal pushes and pulls which move teachers closer to and further from presenting themselves honestly and openly to children. We have caught glimpses of how important the child's reaction can be to a teacher who is grappling with his identity as a facilitator.

Perhaps what many of the above teacher statements indicate is that in the process of interacting with children the teacher leaves himself exposed to children's positive and negative reactions. It often proves difficult for teachers to evaluate their impact on children partly because they are not altogether certain of how they themselves behave and partly because the messages they receive back from the children are either confusing or painfully insightful.

CHILDREN REFLECTING TEACHER BEHAVIORS

Undoubtedly, most teachers desperately want to have an impact on children with whom they deal. When it does happen, and we have reason to believe it may happen more frequently than teachers realize, it may arouse as much discomfort as it does joy. The grip of a teacher on a child may convey conflicting messages from the teacher. It is another in a long series of relationship paradoxes in which a quality of interacting is sought and in fact achieved and then its occurrence is either doubted or agonizingly reinterpreted in consonance with the adult's self concept.

> Helen: I had a little girl who was behaving like she started in September—and I just said, "Kate, go to the door and get your hat and coat." She said, "What? You should be taking me to the door and talking to me!"

One of Helen's goals for much of the school year had been to provide the kind of classroom environment in which this child would internalize some of the teacher's standards for self control. Now here was the child playing back (and perhaps playing with) Helen's exact phraseology! The teacher, in relating this to the group, felt that the child was detecting and reflecting inconsistent teacher behavior.

> Helen: I thought, Oh my gosh! A hit on the head. I thought, Helen, you're being inconsistent. I'd had many other things going and it caught me off guard.

This form of self-confrontation with the child acting as a social mirror can be devastating. And so it was to Helen and to others. When feelings of inadequacy are high, then the interpretation of such imitative behavior on the part of the child can take on negative proportions. "I feel like I'm a failure," was the teacher's response.

> Helen: This happened again today with how they perceive me. It was the end of the day and I had a reading group and a new boy was there. He came in today. Well, I was having trouble getting him there so it ended up that we role-played. Someone was teacher for the lesson. They chose a story and so they had to be me, and boy! It was very interesting, to see how they would handle it and how they perceived me, you know. They gave it to me. They said, "Your turn to read, do you want to read? You feel you don't want to read?" I was thinking—my gosh, they're pretty sophisticated.

Jack: Isn't that interesting that even though we have lots of qualms about ourselves, it's still easier to be top dog, isn't it?

The responsibilities following from awareness of a child's perception of the relationship were highlighted by Betty. She described a situation in which a girl in her class was being prepared for transition back to a regular classroom. Betty told the child that she might have some questions and thoughts she would like to discuss. The child responded by stating that she had something to say, but would write it down.

Betty: What she wrote was, ". . . I'm in my teacher's hands." Perhaps this was her way of saying I have confidence in you. If it had been said a week earlier I would have been completely unable to handle it. I think I would have walked out of the classroom.

Such openness on the part of the child can be disconcerting, even alarming to an unprepared teacher. The implicit need here would be for a meaningful response by a teacher. Self disclosure by a child, in instances like Betty found herself, clearly places the teacher under some obligation to respond and act in helpful ways.

TEACHER OPENNESS

Openness and sharing of one's feelings in reacting to children has been advocated by some as the kind of atmosphere that children need for growth. As with many other relationship stances, this belief in self-disclosure must be considered of value only in the context of what the child or group can respond to without feeling unduly burdened by what the teacher is communicating. Some of the ramifications of such teacher behavior can be seen in the following:

Ken: I was angry and I told them, I should never have told them. It was the first time I ever did it. I just whacked a basketball on the floor, and said, "Knock it off, I'm getting angry!"

         *   *   *

         The first time I did this I got such a reaction back I got scared—I don't get angry anymore.

It became apparent from many of the group discussions that the members were paying a high price for not expressing their "real" feelings. In one discussion of difficult relationship situations, many group members expressed a discrepancy between what they were feeling, i.e., anxiety and fear, and what they actually did in the interaction. Thus, individual teachers felt the risks were high when they engaged in self-disclosure behavior, and just as high when they avoided expressing their feelings.

Mary: Can you outlaw the feeling? Can you say you're not going to be there or are you not going to show it?

Barbara: One of my kids came to class with a hammer the other day and I just had to wait and take it away from him. You can't let them see your fear.

Mary: You can't let them see it, but does that mean you can actually say you're not frightened in a situation? Once I was locked in with six very disturbed kids and a fire started. It didn't dawn on them that the whole thing was cardboard and the whole thing would go up and it got out of control. I was scared, but I couldn't show it. But that feeling was there.

Barbara: Well, that's scared in a different way. I'm speaking of scared of their physical violence and what they would do to you.

Mary: All right, I had a boy put a knife on me who was very hostile. I'm not going to show any fear but I did feel that I've got to handle this. I saw it flashing through my mind.

Helen: I think I would think about what possibly could happen. Knowing if I were to be alone in a room with fourteen or sixteen disturbed boys, I'd have to think through very carefully how I'd handle things to avoid acting a particular way.

The concerns raised by the teachers regarding how open one should be with children presented an approach-avoidance situation. Many of them realized they had far to go before feeling comfortable sharing their deeper feelings and true reactions with children. Others were equally concerned with the ability of children to handle such directness from an adult. Basically, for most of them it meant some basic change in their interaction patterns with children.

TEACHER CHANGE

The theme of whether it is just as necessary for teachers to change and modify their behaviors as it is for children emerged early in the sessions. It was enlightening for some and frightening for others that it may be the teacher who will need to change; that a child's emotional problems do not always lend themselves to quick and easy solutions; and that one has to personally commit oneself to long range efforts at effecting change in both oneself and one's children. Many of us verbalized this stance but Barbara's comment brought such concern alive with feeling.

Barbara: . . . but these kids don't change the next day. Their pattern is still there and it's you that's got to change. The kid hasn't changed any, it's the way you look at the kid that has changed. And this is so true and you know this when you go in. You know, gee, I can't blow it again tomorrow. What am I going to do, how am I going to handle it and why did I feel this way today?

Helen: But why this?

Barbara: Well, you knew good and well you weren't able to handle it that way. You blew it and in my book, and that's the way I feel about it.

Betty: . . . this is an entire dialogue within ourselves, some of the time the questions must be, what is it in me?

Barbara: Open my mind to what I goofed on with that kid today. I didn't say the right thing, I didn't have the right affect.

Ken: You rearrange your self concept when you do this because you have one when you go in and a child challenges it. It doesn't work and you walk out of there and all of a sudden what you thought you were—you're not. And when you get outside that room, you're—wow!

*   *   *

This is where a long ride home does a lot of good because you get in the car and all of a sudden you're—well, I couldn't say you're nobody. You're somebody and you didn't go to school with him in the morning and you know somebody better get out of this car.

Such dialogues brought the group face to face with concern with their need to change in order to help the child. Is this me, do I like what I see? Similarly, the question arose, if I'm going to change, what do I change to if I'm not completely aware of what and who I am as a teacher now? A kind of isolation and estrangement from self and from others fostered powerful feelings of loneliness and raised equally powerful feelings of loneliness and concerns as to whether they could last as teachers faced with such large responsibilities.

LONELINESS

Teachers are constantly chastised for not asking for help and for not asking the "good" questions. Perhaps they find themselves in the bind of not knowing what to ask for, because of the enormous complexity of sorting out who they are and what they do. Coupled with this is the question all need to ask of the educational environment—to whom do teachers go for help and support? The following statement illustrates the dilemma of to whom do teachers turn.

> Betty: What came to my mind when you were talking is what happens to all this feeling inside. I mean, I can remember carrying it around and not talking with anybody about it.

Our group of teachers clearly reflected the range of feelings and emotions often ascribed to loneliness. Moustakas (1961) has said:

> Man is ultimately and forever lonely whether his loneliness is the exquisite pain of the individual living in isolation of illness, the sense of absence caused by a loved one's death, or the piercing joy experienced in triumphant creation. (p. ix)

They were often quick to acknowledge its existence, sometimes reluctant to confront it and always resistant to giving up under its weight and impact. The following dialogue points to how the group viewed loneliness as a group phenomenon as well as an individual reaction.

> Jack: Before we were saying that one of the problems is exposing ourselves to the kids, or just exposing ourselves. Our concern over losing control may be one of the reasons for reluctance to give ourselves away and this makes us feel so vulnerable.
>
> Betty: There's an awful sense of aloneness in this battle too.
>
> Pat: Yes.
>
> Jack: What do you mean, Betty?
>
> Betty: Well, this awful kind of questioning, and there is nobody there with you.
>
> Pat: We're not doing anything right.
>
> Ken: You can't in the school because they just don't accept the level you're in.
>
> Jack: You're not describing just geographical aloneness.
>
> Barbara: It's not easy to live your philosophy.
>
> Will: Barbara, what about you? The rest of us are all in public schools and you're in a treatment center, do you have that same feeling? At least you would think that people there that you know have a little in common with you. What do they do to you there?
>
> Barbara: Well, people still don't understand kids' emotional disturbances. What my kids have done to some of the adults

nobody would believe. And some of the people, you know, still can't accept the acting out behavior. Somebody in my group was saying—what are the kids doing down there? He knows what they are doing down there, but he goes upstairs and takes everybody else's side against me and against the kids. This kind of shook me up because I thought, gee, this is somebody I thought was with me and understood. Everybody hears the kids scream and it echoes though the hallways. A lot of people come up and say, "I don't know how you take it."

Will: All of a sudden that statement takes on a new meaning.

Pat: You feel like they are saying, "What's wrong with you that you take all that crap from those kids?"

Barbara: How sick are you?

Jack: You must be some kind of nut!

Ken: I like, "God bless you."

Pat: Yes, I got that also.

Will: That hit a nerve, didn't it?

Pat: How do you take it with those kids, something about God bless you and it's a shame you have to be with those kids.

Jack: Or better yet, "I think it's wonderful what you're doing."

Barbara: "I could never do it, but I think what you're doing is fine."

Will: "You have so much patience."

The remedy for loneliness remains elusive and there is some question as to whether one is desirable even if attainable. In a rather dramatic way the group discussed how honest and open communication in their group session both contributed to awareness of and reduced their feelings of loneliness.

Jack: You're describing, to say the least, that this has been a very different kind of group meeting.

Barbara: What I felt was that somebody would say something and all of a sudden somebody else would jump in and say the same point. This is what I was getting at, somebody would say something and somebody else would jump in with their point and I know it seemed like we were really communicating.

Will: It seems awfully easy to express your feeling.

Barbara: We were all jumping in the same pond and you know it was comfortable sinking kind of. Now we need artificial respiration.

Betty: First of all we were on land that was sinking—now we're in the water.

Helen: We admit that we're alone, that we're feeling all those feelings of inadequacy.

Mary: But we're alone together now.

Will: I think we know some of the reasons we're alone, don't you?

Helen: Yes, I think we've known the reasons we were alone.

Will: Well, I don't know if I have as clearly as I feel it tonight.

Helen: But we still have the feelings.

Barbara: I feel just through expressing it that it helps. Ken said he dropped back and punted, but I feel like I have a lot more people on my team to drop back and punt with. Sharing feeling and sharing people.

What shapes does loneliness take as it impinges on the classroom life of teachers? To Betty, "It's a kind of desperateness because you're really alone in the kinds of decisions you have to make."

Betty: There are many realizations that cause a sense of loneliness. Part of it is the basic reality that nobody else really knows what it's like to live in that room besides you and that is something that is going all the time.

And another kind of loneliness is that you get the sense of being tested. Who else is out there that knows what you're talking about? And to whom do you talk if a person can look in and tell you very easily what to do?

And then there's the kind of loneliness of newness too. You know, you've never been in this particular situation. You've never worked within these certain limitations. Then there's another kind of loneliness that can easily be misunderstood, so that I don't even know whether to say it, but sometimes you do get a feeling that there's nobody else around who can read the kids' behavior any better than you can and that's the kind of loneliness that eats at you. It isn't even that kind of loneliness, you know, it isn't a physical kind of thing because there's people around and there's kids. Well, in one part you view something that is crumbling around you to the point that you have to build out every layer of ground before you and the group take a step on it because everything that is solid you and the group have to build. Nothing is there for you, and you're exhausted by building all those steps by Tuesday, and by Wednesday it crumbles. You build it, you step, and it's gone and you do it again.

Will: We haven't said who we feel lonely from, for example. It's only that if you feel lonely, it's almost like there's an implication that there should be some kind of a way of not being lonely and that's usually by those that you work with or that you associate with. In the cases you're bringing up, you're in a different world in your classes as compared with the other people who work in a public school.

Mary: You're surrounded by people who don't understand and refuse to understand.

Many in our group felt that they were going it alone. The above quotations illustrate their concerns over being misperceived, or even more devastating, not being perceived at all. The following statement by Helen is a report of her end of the year evaluation conducted by her building principal and supervisor of special education. It was a very negative encounter for her, but one in which she struggled bravely to maintain her integrity as a person.

Helen: They were questioning my whole philosophy of working with children. He said, "If we bring visitors into your room, you don't look like a good teacher, the classroom doesn't look like a good class, and this is what you have to attain. You have to present an image and the children to present an image," and I looked at him and I said to him, "You're sure this is what you want to say?" And then he questioned philosophy and what he was saying is that feelings shouldn't be dealt with and they should learn to park them at the door. In other words—you can come in, Johnny, but leave your feelings at the door.
Well, they said to me at a point, this was after an hour and a half, they said, we feel there has to be a certain change for what we want in the program. We don't want you to feel too uncomfortable. I said, all right, you can stop right there, you have my answer, I won't be here next year. I believe in the way I work and the philosophy I have —I think I would be uncomfortable making the changes. I agree with you, this is what you have and this is the way you perceive the program to be and if you believe in it, look for a different person. I agree with you, I should be somebody else, so the next hour and a half was building Helen up and—
I know you changed something but I'm bringing it up because we were talking about it at a meeting and there was very strong feeling about it. I was then called in after school was out by the administrator of the building who seemed very anxious. He wanted to know why I thought and why I reacted, and when I named off ten criticisms in every area, and he said—"no, no, I don't want you to feel like this," he said. "I like you so much as a person." And I said, "I don't care, don't like me as a person. I want you to like me as a teacher, you know, respect me as a teacher. I don't care what you think of me as a person," which he couldn't react to, and I got it from this meeting because we were talking about exactly that and how it affected us.

Perhaps on the basis of the above dialogue between Helen and her principal we can finally lay to rest some of the cliches we have grown fond of. When her principal told her that he liked her as a person but not as a teacher, it was reminiscent of what we say to children—we like you but not your behavior. Some professional workers feel there is something very conditional about such a message and that is how Helen reacted. The kinds of controls and possessiveness acted out toward Helen concerned our teachers with their own behavior toward children. They desperately wanted to avoid manipulating what children could and couldn't do in classrooms. The freedom they sought for themselves was what they hoped they could provide for their children.

NON-POSSESSIVE PRESENTATION OF SELF

In many ways our teachers saw themselves behaving in a possessive fashion, not unlike the parent behaviors they often described.

Ken: . . . When you're involved with the whole school and a child gets in trouble with another teacher, you go right up and stop it. And when he's in the gym or cafeteria, you have it put before you. The child is in there and he's on his own and he's interacting with other teachers. But if you don't have a chance to do that and you don't have a chance for the child to move out in the school environment other than the one you set up, he becomes almost an extension of you. You expect him to act as you would, and when you see a situation, bear down on him. You're standing there trying to get him to think and do what you'd do and it becomes frightening when you're trying to live for that child. You're almost trying to send messages to him. You're thinking for him what he should be doing and watching him.

How to let go of the reins with what child and under which conditions is a question of great interpersonal and strategic concern. The enormous feelings of hopelessness and despair generated by the behavior and affect of our pupils are often fueled by our possessive behavior toward them. Our group meetings, however, pointed up the complexity behind teachers' avoidance of possessive intentions in the classroom. In far too many situations a successful teacher is one who controls his classroom. Schools often begin with the assumption that controls need to be externally induced and constantly reiterated. This group of teachers, however, were in the process of formulating their ideas about helping the child build internalized sets of controls.

WHO'S IN CHARGE?

Many teachers are quick to state that their first task in the classroom is to let the child know who the boss is. One gets the impression of some kind of race for classroom leadership, a feeling that if the teacher doesn't get there first the children will. And so it goes. The explicit assertion is that as controls are established there will be a lessening of teacher domination. In practice this may prove to be an unfounded assumption. This "boss theory" of relating has not been a productive one but rather has fostered possessiveness. The message that is communicated is that of "I will set the tone and pattern for behavior by what I say. You watch and listen so you can replicate it." Our group was intrigued with another possibility which was verbalized by Barbara.

Barbara: Isn't this the point when we become real ego involved and you let the child use your ego to a certain extent?

Several group members wanted to behave as well as verbalize in ways which would foster individual initiative. They were willing to "loan" parts of themselves out to the children, but only for as long as they were needed. Such a stance is not without its difficulties, as seen in the following dialogue:

Helen: I don't know how to handle what's coming next because of all of this.
Betty: Where do you leave off and he begin? Where do you leave off and where does he begin?
Helen: I'm just plain cutting off with him now.
Betty: Is that saying anything to you?
Helen: No.
Ken: Do you think that child could do anything on his own right now?
Helen: Well, he is doing things on his own.
Ken: Without your influence?
Helen: Well, you can't say without my influence because I'm there. I don't know how much is my influence.
Ken: Can you cut off if he gets in trouble outside the classroom? Suppose he comes down and he gets into trouble with me or something?
Barbara: Then he'd have to handle it.

Ken sums up his position rather clearly when he states:

When they are in the midst of your program and they are going to be there for two years, and it's mid-year the first year or the end of the first year and all of a sudden you start thinking of him as something besides an independent person, I think you are in deep trouble then.

Mary states how much difficulty she had in doing what Ken suggests and the price she paid for possessive behavior:

Oh, I just felt like at the end of the year I had accomplished absolutely nothing because I'd become so involved. I just felt with the kids too much. I was too busy understanding the way they felt and feeling sorry for them and doing this for them and doing that for them and getting absolutely nothing accomplished, absolutely nothing.

How individual teachers resolve the dilemma of closeness without possessiveness is of importance both to themselves and in guiding their future interactions with children. Shortly after Mary made the above comment in session four, she indicated one solution she actively considered:

Mary: It's more than objectivity, it's a real distance that you just keep there and it's hard to explain.
Jack: You mean it's a struggle to hold it in focus?
Mary: It is. That's right.
Helen: What do you mean by distance?
Mary: You know what's going on all the time, but you don't become overly involved with them. You must remember that you are the teacher, you are not the parent, you are not the sister, you are not the brother, you're not even the doctor, and you're not the therapist.

There is a plaintive ring to Mary's statement, particularly in light of the powerful figures she lists—parents, doctors, therapists—and exclusion of teachers from playing those roles. The issue of teachers not wanting to be possessive toward children, but at the same time questioning the lack of power or impact they had with children remained a gnawing concern.

POWERLESSNESS

Powerlessness as a theme had bubbled throughout the early sessions and surfaced around the discussion of teachers seeing themselves through children's behavior. Pat was involved in a special class program, in which she had a group for only the morning. In the afternoon they returned to a regular classroom with another teacher. During a discussion of children's imitative reactions to teachers, several of the group members expressed their concern over why their children behaved better in other classroom situations than in theirs. This was particularly upsetting to them in the light of the rather possessive feelings they had for the welfare and improvement of their children. Pat indicated that kids often became very controlled with other teachers and she stated, "and you don't happen to be there, which is something that happens to me every day and I don't think I've quite learned how to live with it yet." Pat was directly implying that when her group was with her, they evidenced considerably less control, in contrast to the time when they returned next door to the regular classroom setting.

Ken related a discussion he had with a youngster about his acting-out behavior. "I said, 'Would you do this now in a regular class?' He said, 'no,' and it infuriated me. I said, 'What did you do it to me for?' That was just about the tone of voice I used," Ken said.

We can see from these two examples that Pat and Ken were close to communicating to the child that they, as teachers, were demanding certain patterns of behavior and certain responses because of their own strong feelings and needs. In other words, the message of, "Do it for me," tended to permeate a good deal of their response patterns as they became more interpersonally involved with the children and began to be more connected with their own feelings and anxieties about their relationships with the children.

As we might expect, powerful feelings of possessiveness enhance the likelihood that one will perceive the slightest infraction of the rules as a personal insult. If one maintains this degree of possessiveness, then everything that is done is directed at the giver, in this instance the teachers.

Pat relates the following:

> I get the feeling, well, you know, if they don't need to do it in the afternoon, why do they need to do it here? I know why they need to do it in here, okay, but it's like, you know, maybe it happened to you today and maybe it happened to you some other time—it happens to me every single day, so you multiply that. You multiply what happened once by how many days we've been in school and you have poor mental health on the part of the teacher.

Pat goes on to say:

> You know, you're up on this hill and everybody in the whole school is saying, 'Look, look,' and you're all there for six months and you're saying, 'Well, yes,' but then after six months you finally say, 'Yes,

what is it?' I don't know, I think I just finally came to the point and it's like they've got you, you know.

Her expectation was that she and the children would be on display for quite a bit of time but that after sufficient time, things would be shaped up and they would not be nearly as visible to the entire school in terms of acting out behavior. She related a great sense of frustration at the fact that after an extended block of time, much of the children's deviant behavior was still visible, particularly when they were with her, even if it subsided with other teachers.

Such feelings of responsibility at some point lead to anger. Pat states, "You know, we get the message all the time that we should take that kid and shake him, knock him up against the wall, and he won't do it again. What that kid needs is a good spanking. Why do you take all that from them? They don't need it. You should see how well they behave when they get a substitute."

ANGER AND ACTION

As feelings of possessiveness get stronger, and are coupled with feelings of anger, what begins to happen is a feeling on the part of the teacher that he is being repaid for his kindness and concern with sabotage on the part of the child. Some members of our teacher group expressed the feeling that they didn't feel the child was being honest, that they were conned by children and that the children were not able to understand or grasp what the teachers were attempting to accomplish.

In rather dramatic ways the genuine involvement of many of the group members continued to surface and was reflected in their constant searching for the basis for their predicament and what they could do about it.

Betty: But what is it that makes us question? What makes us feel we don't know what we're doing? I don't know what we're doing at all. Then I don't know what I'm doing, where does this come from? Does it come from what we see or do? Or does it come from, you know, weariness? Does it come from loneliness and depression?

Ken: A split second when you get the old behavior and you start through the "what did you do in September" kind of thinking to yourself, when you see the old behavior pop up. You start the same pattern of working that you used in September and he doesn't need that.

As the sessions progressed, several of the teachers sought to diminish their concern with possessiveness by focusing more on what they considered to be realistic goal-setting for the child and reasonable expectations for themselves.

Betty: Yes, what's with you and Larry now?

Helen: He's doing great. He's doing great, I just enjoy him so much; no really, it's nice when a kid looks up and you can really enjoy him.

Betty: What has happened since that time when part of the feeling was where do I stop and then begin kind of thing?

Helen: What happened? I became more relaxed after the session. I had become so anxious and involved. And so I decided I didn't need to worry about the mother. Although the phone calls were coming in and everything was the same, I just concentrated on Larry and working with him in the classroom, and being much more honest with him and giving him more independence in decision making.

Barbara: What do you mean by more honest with him? I mean that night you sounded pretty honest.

Helen: Oh, straightforward with him.

Barbara: Was it more honest or—

Helen: Candid—I began talking to him, putting it on the line. I'd like to say I stopped using kid gloves, would you know what that meant?

Betty: No.

Helen: I mean, I don't know how to say it, and then at the same time I started a different approach with the mother and building up to the mother in weekly conferences the healthiness of the boy because this is what I had to work on because she sees him and she wants him to be a sick boy. And so I started working on that with the mother. And then positive changes started with the boy. He's at the point now where we've got him set for partial integration in a regular fourth grade. We work on his schedule, he can handle all situations, he can interact with peers with no anger at all and if it is, it's been the right way. He can verbalize problems at home and at school, and there is no bizarre behavior at all. I can't believe it's the same boy in so short a time, and I think we have a very good comfortable relationship. I'm more relaxed.

Betty: It's interesting, one of the things you said was you put more decisions to him, more independence.

Helen: Yes, because I remembered that night you were saying, where do you leave off and give him a chance to begin? And then I started noticing myself, I was very observant, I was very calm—aware of what I did. I'd start to say something in the hall, and then I'd say, I don't have to do this, you know, this is what they mean. This is what I'm doing and so I start backing off.

Betty: Yes, but it's almost as though, you know, one way to find out how separate we are is to see the kinds of decisions you can handle, see how they can handle you—that's what I meant.

Barbara: Could you have done this in September?

Helen: Oh, I had to go through, we had to go through all that. Let's say this, at the time I spoke the last time I was very confused and very unsure of what I had and of the steps I had taken because of the steps or the stages Larry was going through and the behavior he was showing. But now looking back over everything, behavior records and everything, I think that it couldn't have been any other way. I think that the uncomfortableness had to be felt and he had to show the behavior he was showing to go on, and what got me upset was the mother making me feel guilty if I said something or causing something that maybe hadn't been there before and until I sat down and really thought what am I working with in the home, what type of home is this, things didn't get better.

There is much contained in this dialogue between Helen and the others. At an earlier session she had described, with great despair, her inability to even begin to cope with Larry. What is described above is a newly found sense of purpose and direction. To a great extent, once she had come to grips with her rather strong feelings of possessiveness, she was then able to step back and look at both her contribution to the relationship and the kinds of life forces impinging on Larry. She felt better able to look at the psycho-social stages through which he was progressing; at her own intolerance for ambiguity; the impact of the mother's behavior on both child and teacher; and her own angry feelings toward the mother for subverting the good things she felt she was doing. In contrast to focusing solely on what teacher strategy was being employed, Helen began to focus on the decisions each of them could and should make and "being much more honest with him." From the tone of her statements, she was beginning to feel considerably unburdened, based largely on her realization that a relationship should be the responsibility of both teacher and child. She more clearly saw her role as a facilitative one, aided by an approach in which she represented herself honestly and non-possessively.

Helen's resolve to respond in facilitative ways was one the others supported for themselves. But like many other good intentions there were some phases in their relationships with children that severely taxed their interpersonal resources. One such phase was that of physically separating from the children.

IDENTIFICATION AND SEPARATION

One of the most dramatic paradoxes of an intense teacher-child interaction environment has to do with the child's improvement and subsequent need to separate from the teacher in order to independently consolidate his newly developed skills. Despite the many admonitions to the contrary, they had likely received during training and on the job, these teachers found themselves operating from the heart and not the mind. Several of them identified rather totally with the child and his problems. While their goal was certainly one of fostering the child's independence, the intensity of the relationship made the separation an ambivalent one.

Barbara: The feeling to me is the intensity in which we work with these kids. We've got a smaller number of kids and we get intensely involved with them. You knew Larry when you talked to him about his behavior, backwards, forwards and sideways, now suddenly this kid you knew every way he moves, has changed, and this is to me what we are talking about. We're talking about a changed kid that is ready to move on.

Betty: You know, once he needed me so much but now he's out there.

Betty later went on to elaborate in rather plaintive terms how much she felt the children needed them.

Betty: I still think it hurts to know and believe that once this kid had to have you to survive in a day, you know, needed your ego to even function, now you really can't do anything.

Of interest in her comment is her notion that what contributed to the helping process was the sharing of one's ego. The giving of a slice of oneself seems to commit both the teacher and child. The givers, in these instances the teachers, were apparently left with perceptions of seeing themselves in the actions of the child. Our group of teachers felt that a resolution could only come about through accurate self knowledge of one's own motivational pattern.

Barbara: Well, like Helen was saying at one point with Larry that she was all ego involved and we were telling her at that session that Larry took her ego home. As she says, she started letting Larry make decisions on his own. She said out in the hall I start to say this, she could let Larry's own ego take over without really overburdening him with her own. Now some people can't do this and this is at the point where we need to ask where is your motivation, where do you let the kids take off and where do you step off to?

The logical outcome of such an intertwining of teacher and child was seen in teacher investment in the child's need to do well as he was phased out of a special class into regular classroom. After all, it wasn't just the child who would be judged by the rest of the staff, but his teacher as well.

Helen: Yes, this one boy that has gone back, he's in there full time now and he doesn't need to come around to me anymore to say hello. And he doesn't. He hangs his coat up and he doesn't even bother to look. For awhile he looked every day; when he went streaming by without waving and for awhile—gosh darn, he made it so easy—he's doing it easier than me.

The powerful feelings surrounded final separation of a group from a teacher are poignantly reported by Ken.

Ken: I told them that I'd be leaving at the end of the year. "What day and the date," they asked and that started it. That was the first question. Then, "Do you want to go?" And I talked for awhile and couldn't get out of it. I just said no, I don't, and stopped explaining it because it was as much as I could say. And I had to just say no and sometimes I picked up kind of a smirk or something. I just asked them then, "Do you want to go?" and they said, "no." I feel the same way but it's coming in from all sides. The year is ending, the kids are going upstairs and when they leave I don't know what to do either. I don't want to say congratulations and I don't want to say stay here and just tell them, you know, this is what we worked for. I'm happy to see you go or, I'd like you to stay, and I don't know how it comes through, and it's just their very walking out of the room somewhat to say to them when they go out, so nine times out of ten I shut up because I don't know how to explain it to them.

Ken is moved to relate his observation that the "out of sight, out of mind" phenomenon seems to apply to their work with these children.

Ken: Some of the kids, if you met them at Green Lakes and started to talk about last September, you'd better be in shallow water because that was a different person. I don't know, you just don't talk about that anymore. If they refer to it, all right, and you know that's as far as they want to go. You can refer back to, you know, well, we solved that alright or we worked through that or we did this, but that's it.

Perhaps what is being suggested is that, in effect, the children want us to forget them. Even when we have an impact while they are with us, once gone we are reminders of a time in their life that they would just as soon forget about. This possibility was difficult to accept for many in the group. It was one harsh reality among a multitude of realities that severely taxed the teacher's understanding of what was happening and how to respond with understanding and accuracy to the expressed and implied messages of children.

EMPATHIC RESPONSES OF TEACHERS

At some point it will become necessary for those of us heavily invested in the preparation of teachers to critically analyze some of the concepts we have long believed important. The importance of teachers being accurately empathic has been and is gaining widespread interest and attention. This group of teachers, interestingly enough, suffered from an overactive empathic concern.

Betty: . . . and I can't help but feel, you know, do any of us really know what it's like to come from what they come from? I've learned from some of the kids that I work with more than any books or anything I've read.

Where does Betty's statement leave us? For some teachers this is a clear mandate to psychologically flee the scene. Others will attempt to utilize empathic concern as an intervention. Betty tried this on for size, but was only partially convinced.

Betty: . . . One way of talking with youngsters where a lot of feeling is involved when you're dealing individually is to convey empathy to the youngster within the situation and I think we are extremely limited here.
Jack: What do you mean by extremely limited?
Betty: Well, I would be. I don't know what I'd really know. I can guess at the hurt that goes on, you know, and I can feel in a way for the kids, but I imagine it would be much more beyond that.

IMPLICATIONS FOR MOVING CLOSE TO CHILDREN

Some children's life experiences are so harsh and beyond the comprehension of adults that more exposure to what the child is experiencing may be insufficient. Far too often many of us operate on the assumption that teachers lack factual information about how their children live outside of school. The description which follows, offered by Pat, should alert us to how difficult it can be to integrate such "objective" information with the emotional involvement and intensity of teachers and their relationships with the children.

Pat: So today was the first time that I was without meetings, and I was able to have him stay after school, and then take him home, and oh, it was really terrible. I took him home and there is this river area by town where all the houses or shacks or whatever you want to call them are. Middle class people might say that they will do for a summer place but these are places where people live all year long. And there are eleven people in Roger's family and his house was down this muddy dirt road with all kinds of ruts and water. A two room house, unpainted, that was just—oh, I don't know. To see this and see all these other houses in the area and knowing that Roger also lives in this area, it was like—I had a physical reaction, kind of sick—it was really terrible. And you know I kind of left him off down from his house. And he told me to stop but then I had to turn around so I watched where he went and I know that the house had a stove in the middle because the kids come to school with burns on their arms and other places because they touch this pot-bellied stove. I try to talk to the other kids about, you know, their attacks on this boy because they are different and I really don't think I understood it until today. It had such an impact to see where this child exists and I think what it really made me wonder is what can you really do about the kids that are coming from this place. If you were driving along and you saw an unpainted board building, you would think, "now, somebody keeps their tools in there," but people really lived in it, and I'm really hung up on that. I had to get out of the house after I got home because I didn't want to think about it. But you know, it presents, I think, a problem. What do you do about a kid like this? How much can you really feel you know what he's feeling, how can you really know about what his life is like and trying to picture it. I can imagine Roger in this apartment, being you know, just overwhelmed by everything and very ill at ease, and all kinds of behavior that Redl described when he took one of his pioneers to one of the Junior League member's homes and how they, you know, just really couldn't use anything appropriately. I hadn't thought that much about it but it just happened today and what's been going on in the classroom is talking with the children and when it goes too far the instigator is put out of the room which has done a lot of good for Arthur and Robert because when this happens, when somebody says, "Oh, you're a welfare case," or something like that and it continues and the person goes out of the room after they have been warned, I get behaviors from Arthur like—oh, well, we can look at the same reading book today or I'm going to sit by you at lunch. Things like this they let me know that, you know, they come right after I've said, "Okay, you go out of the room because we can't hurt people with words," but I think the real thing that bothers me is, you know, what can you do?

Jack: So really we're in the business of understanding children and of course we have to continually interpret to them that we do understand and you're raising the question of do we really understand.

Pat: How can you know how it feels to be very cold every night and to not have anything to eat and to come in, you know, with rotten dirty clothes?

Feeling for and with children may serve to make some teachers feel impotent to assist children. Pat's reaction comes close to such feelings. She wondered aloud at what could really be done by someone as middle class as she when the child's environment is every bit as bad as she says it is. For this teacher at least, seeing it was not to believe it. It was culture shock that raised for Pat the major questions of whether she could be facilitative in her relationship with Henry when she was so far from understanding his particular set of life circumstances.

We need to ask just how much do we have to experience to be facilitative in our classroom relationships with children. Is it necessary to be slightly schizophrenic to work with schizophrenics? Does one have had to come up through poverty in order to know how a child may react to such an experience? Some of our teachers felt the answer was yes to these questions, particularly when they had been profoundly affected by a new reality in a child's life. They raised the valid question of how accurate an empathic mirror they could raise to the child so that he could experience his feelings more accurately.

SUMMARY

This chapter has attempted to capture the flavor of teacher-child relationships as reported by our group of teachers. The broad interpersonal concerns of authenticity, loneliness, nonpossessiveness, and empathy were discussed, primarily using the words and feelings of the teachers. Their eloquence in expressing themselves is evidence for their depth of involvement with children and their ongoing struggle to gain awareness of themselves as persons and teachers.

The dilemma of generating authentic behavior toward children when one is unsure of many facets of one's own feelings was constantly with our group. It must be remembered that such self-doubt is not always irrational or even unjustified, particularly if we consider how difficult and complex the children were with whom these teachers interacted day after day. Slight chinks in one's interpersonal stance could create much anguish between child and teacher. Of particular interest was the interpersonal sensitivity and awareness displayed by many children toward their teachers.

As we saw it, one of the core problems faced by teachers was that of loneliness. In many ways, teachers of troubled children have been abandoned by other school staff members. It may not always be a process of conscious exclusion, but rather a lack of awareness and understanding of the difficulty of the task faced by such teachers. There may also be a pulling away by the teachers themselves from other staff members whom they perceive, accurately or otherwise, to be hostile to their efforts. This group of teachers talked of how closely involved they were with children in their classes, but longed for broader and more meaningful contacts with other adults.

Perhaps the feelings of loneliness added to our teachers' concern over how possessive they felt toward children. They felt involved, protective and responsible for their children. They were ambivalent over their close feelings for children, and wondered at what point did they become too involved.

Of equal concern were their feelings that perhaps they couldn't be of substantial assistance to children in difficulty because they couldn't get close enough to the problems the children lived with. Or if they did get close, they couldn't understand the distorted life experiences of some children.

Much of the content reported in this chapter leaves one with the feeling of being on an interpersonal roller coaster. The ups and downs are dramatic and often unpredictable. We could see our group of teachers agonize over one aspect of their interactions with children and feel very good over other aspects. However, one must come away from our meetings with a deep sense of the seriousness with which these teachers faced their jobs. One cannot help but be impressed with their genuine interest in increasing their awareness and skills, and in the basically hopeful feelings they have about the capacity of children to grow.

It is our hope that this book has demonstrated the need for the development of group processes within which teachers could acquire the skills, attitudes, and behaviors necessary to facilitate positive interactions with children and adults. The many forces operating within a school and which necessitate our viewing the school as a social system present teachers with potential barriers against obtaining adequate gratifications as facilitators of children's learning and adjustment. Our feeling is that the growth potential of teachers, just as with children, is unlimited, and that the development of group process approaches is one design in which such teacher potential can be realized.

REFERENCE

Moustakas, C. E. *Loneliness.* (Englewood Cliffs, N.J.: Prentice-Hall, 1961).

Appendix

Psychological Testing

We have sought in the preceding chapters to describe the nature of our teacher group from a variety of perspectives. Continuing in this direction, the present section briefly reports the results of psychological testing conducted during the course of the group's development. Consistent with the overriding relationship focus of our group's goals, the intent of our test battery in broadest terms was to discern (1) the nature of and changes in member-to-member relationships over time, (2) changes in member's views of themselves as functioning teachers and their characteristic relationships with their pupils, and (3) the manner in which their pupils viewed them.

The Teacher-Pupil Relationship Inventory (TPRI) was the major instrument utilized. Historically, this measure grew from investigations of the therapist-patient relationship in psychotherapy. Originally initiated by Fiedler (1950), and subsequently developed and revised in studies by Heine (1950), Snyder (1961), Ashby, et al. (1957), Goldstein (1970) and others, it has by now come to have considerable construct validity associated with it. Lewis, et al. (1965) in an attempt to adapt these test items for usage in a teacher-pupil context, cite evidence to suggest that: ". . . the good therapeutic relationship is not unique to therapy, but can be matched in interpersonal relationships that do not have a stated goal of therapy." (p. 396) With this as their broad rationale, they tested and successfully demonstrated that ". . . those students who perceive a relationship with their teacher that is in the direction of the ideal psychotherapeutic relationship . . . will make greater academic gains . . . than those students who perceive a non-therapeutic relationship with their teacher." (p. 397) Thus,

143

Lewis et al. have provided an important increment to the construct validity of these test items in general, and the TPRI in particular. Table 2 below is a listing of the original, psychotherapy-oriented test items developed by Heine; the TPRI statements developed by Lewis et al. for pupils to respond to, items which we adapted so that our teachers could respond to them under varying instructional sets; and our modification of these items for usage with disturbed third and fourth grade pupils (Lewis et al.'s sample were non-disturbed sixth graders).

TABLE 2   TPRI statements

Psychotherapy	Teachers	Pupils
1. The therapist never let me feel that he rather than I was to take responsibility for solving my problems.	1. The teacher always lets me feel that I was to take responsibility for what I learned.	1. The teacher always lets me figure out my school work.
2. It seemed to me that the therapist didn't take his work too seriously.	2. It seemed to me that the teacher didn't take his work very seriously.	2. The teacher is a hard worker.
3. The therapist got across the feeling that we were really working together to understand my problem.	3. The teacher got across the feeling that we were really working together to help me learn.	3. The teacher made me feel we were working together.
4. There was definitely a feeling of mutual trust in my relations with the therapist.	4. I felt sure that I could trust the teacher and he seemed to feel that he could trust me.	4. The teacher and I trust each other.
5. The therapist seemed to want me to maintain pretty close control over my emo-	5. The teacher seemed not to want me to show it when I was very happy	5. The teacher didn't want me to show when I was happy or sad.

Psychotherapy	*Teachers*	*Pupils*
tions when I was with him.	or sad.	
6. I had the feeling the therapist was so sympathetic that he couldn't really be helpful.	6. I had the feeling that the teacher was so sympathetic that he couldn't really be helpful.	6. The teacher was kind but couldn't really help me.
7. The therapist was a very natural, unaffected sort of person.	7. The teacher was very natural. He did not try to be like someone else.	7. The teacher acted just like himself, sort of natural.
8. Aside from anything else, the therapist was a likable fellow.	8. Without thinking about anything else, the teacher was a likable person.	8. The teacher was a likable person.
9. I somehow caught the feeling that the therapist couldn't regard me as an equal.	9. I somehow caught the feeling that the teacher couldn't think of me as an equal.	9. The teacher thought he was better than me.
10. It seemed as if the therapist always lapsed into wordy explanations when he might have let me finish.	10. It seemed as if the teacher always started wordy explanations when he might have let me finish.	10. The teacher always talked a lot and didn't let me finish what I wanted to say.
11. I had the feeling that there was one person I could really trust.	11. I had the feeling that here was one person I could really trust.	11. I felt I could really trust my teachers.
12. I never had the feeling that the therapist really understood what I was trying to get across.	12. I never had the feeling that the teacher really understood what I was trying to get across.	12. I never felt that the teacher really understood what I was trying to say and do.

Psychotherapy	Teachers	Pupils
13. The therapist always seemed to know what I was trying to get across to him.	13. The teacher always seemed to know what I was trying to get across to him.	13. The teacher always knew what I was trying to do.
14. The therapist often seemed to be lost in his own thoughts rather than attending to what I said.	14. The teacher often seemed to be lost in his own thoughts rather than thinking about what I said.	14. The teacher often paid more attention to what he was thinking than to what I said.
15. I never had the feeling that the therapist was in over his depth in trying to help me.	15. I had the feeling that the teacher knew what he was doing in trying to teach me.	15. I had the feeling that the teacher always knew what he was trying to teach me.
16. The therapist was anything but cold and distant.	16. It was easy to talk to the teacher. He seemed interested.	16. It was easy to talk to the teacher. He seemed interested.
17. I always had the feeling that I was just another patient as far as the therapist was concerned.	17. I always had the feeling that I was just another student as far as the teacher was concerned.	17. I felt the teacher didn't really like me.
18. I often felt, "I'd better not tell the therapist that."	18. I often felt, "I'd better not tell the teacher that."	18. There were many things I really couldn't tell the teacher.
19. The therapist seemed to be in pretty good control of himself at all times.	19. The teacher seemed to be in pretty good control of himself at all times.	19. The teacher hardly ever lost his temper.
20. I was a little afraid really to tell the therapist what I thought about myself.	20. I was a little afraid really to tell the teacher what I thought about myself and the class.	20. I was a little afraid to tell the teacher what I was feeling about myself and the class.

Immediately following both the fifth and fifteenth group sessions, each group member completed the following version of the TPRI:

1. *TPRI-Self.* Test instructions requested the teacher to indicate the degree to which each item was characteristic of her typical classroom behavior.

2. *TPRI-Ideal.* Test instructions requested the teacher to indicate the degree to which each item was characteristic of her view of the ideal teacher's typical classroom behavior.

3. *TPRI-Other.* Test instructions requested the teacher to indicate, for each member of the group separately, the degree to which each item was probably characteristic of the given member's typical classroom behavior.

4. *TPRI-Pupil.* Test instructions requested the teacher to indicate the degree to which each item was probably characteristic of the way in which her pupils would rate her typical classroom behavior.

The pupil version of the TPRI was completed by all students in each group member's class. This testing took place between the fifth and sixth group meeting and could not be repeated, as the testing of teachers was, due to substantial changes in class enrollment over the intervening weeks.

Scores obtained on these five tests, as well as relevant difference scores, were then intercorrelated, as presented in Table 3.

Several of the correlations presented in Table 2 are instructive with regard to both member and group-wide dimensions. Note, for example, that teacher self and ideal self scores correlate .75 at the fifth session, but only .04 at the fifteenth. Inspection of the actual test scores revealed that this decrease in self-ideal correlation is attributable to changes over the intervening ten sessions in both self and ideal self, but primarily the former. Thus, it seems likely, the ways in which the group's interactions put the members in closer touch with themselves and their problems was reflected primarily in decreasing "self-satisfaction" and increasing awareness of a gap between current functioning and (a relatively stable) aspiration level.

The manner in which a given member was viewed by the rest of the group at the fifth session testing (pre-average rating from other teachers) correlated only .47 with teachers' fifth session view of themselves, but .96 with how they viewed themselves by the fifteenth session. Thus, as our session by session analysis frequently illustrated,

148

TABLE 3 — Test score intercorrelations

	1	2	3	4	5	6	7	8	9	10	11	12	13	14
1. Pre-self		.75	.39	.47	.86	.14	−.39	.46	.40	.08	.35	−.01	−.73	.10
2. Pre-ideal			−.31	.59	.51	.07	−.26	.67	.27	.31	.30	.25	−.30	−.04
3. Pre-self-ideal discrepancy				−.14	.53	.10	−.19	−.25	.20	−.33	.08	−.36	−.62	.19
4. Pre-average rating from other teachers					−.03	.72	−.14	.96	−.15	.83	.59	.19	.23	.02
5. Pre-discrepancy between self and average rating from other teachers						−.25	−.36	−.03	.54	−.39	.09	−.12	.96	.10
6. Pre-average rating from pupils							−.39	.73	−.07	.60	.65	−.06	.41	.29
7. Pre-discrepancy between actual and expected ratings from pupils								−.17	.02	−.14	−.79	.71	.29	−.88
8. Post-self									.04	.73	.51	.32	.27	−.05
9. Post-ideal										−.65	−.45	.52	−.40	−.45
10. Post-self-ideal discrepancy											.70	−.12	.48	.27
11. Post-average rating from other teachers												−.65	.16	.82
12. Post-discrepancy between self and average rating from teachers													.26	−.94
13. Pre-post self discrepancy														.24
14. Pre-post discrepancy in average rating from other teachers														

* P .05 = .707
** Pre = 5th session testing
*** Post = 15th session testing

over the course of the group meetings the members came to view themselves increasingly as the other members viewed them. While this finding may be attributable to a group pressure phenomenon, similar correlations between their pupils' views of the teachers and fifth session (.14) and fifteenth session (.73) teacher views of themselves seems less adequately explainable on an interpersonal basis.

The changing nature of the group over sessions is also evidenced by the shift in correlation between ratings from other teachers and self-ideal discrepancy from the fifth to fifteeenth sessions. The early correlation is —.14, the later one is .70. Apparently, it is the seeming self-assured group member who is viewed most favorably by his peers early in the course of the group. The member behaviorally evidencing greater self-ideal discrepancy, by expressing self-doubts, problems, etc., is less favorably viewed at this early point in time. As the group progressed, the reverse became increasingly true and, as the correlations reflect, introspection, admission and exploration of one's concerns as a teacher and as a person became positively viewed. The apparency of self-assurance, in contrast, apparently came to be interpreted as akin to defensiveness, denial, or as in other ways negative.

The correlation of –.94 between the pre-post difference in ratings from the other teachers and the difference between the post-ratings of this type and the teacher's post-self score is also of interest. The members viewed with increasing favorableness from pre- to post-measurement are those who, at the time of post-measurement, have a small discrepancy between their view of themselves and how others see them. Those who see themselves much more favorably or much less favorably than others see them are not viewed differently by the others on the two measurement occasions.

Finally, and in some ways most interestingly, we note a correlation of .72 between the pre-ratings from the group members and the pre-ratings from the pupils. Both the teacher's peers and pupils view each teacher in a highly similar manner. This finding underscores the consistency of interpersonal evaluations across contexts, and futhermore yields implicit support for the notion that seeking to alter teacher behavior in the group setting can yield corresponding changes in the classroom.

REFERENCES

Ashby, J. D., Ford, D. H., Guerney, B. G., Jr., & Guerney, L. Effects on clients of a reflective and a leading type of psychotherapy, *Psychological Monographs*, 1957, 7, 1–32.

Fiedler, F. W. The concept of the ideal therapeutic relationships, *Journal of Consulting Psychology*, 1950, **41**, 239–243.

Goldstein, A. P. *Psychotherapeutic attraction* (New York: Pergamon Press, 1970).

Heine, R. W. An investigation of the relationship between changes and responsible factors as seen by clients following treatment by psychotherapists of the psychoanalytic, Adlerian and non-directive schools (Unpublished doctoral dissertation, University of Chicago, 1950).

Lewis, W. A., Lovell, J. T., & Jessee, B. E. Interpersonal relationship and pupil progress, *Personnel Guidance Journal*, 1965, **XLIV**, 396–401.

Snyder, W. V. *The psychotherapy relationship* (New York: Macmillan, 1961).

Author Index

Subject Index

Anger, teacher, 133-36
Authenticity, 115-20

Behavioral expectations, 9

Change agent, teacher as, 117
Change:
  in schools, 17-18
  in teachers, 123-24
Cohesiveness, 79, 84, 86, 90, 96
  consequences of, 47-48, 90
Communication:
  adults, 11-14
  subgroups, 16
Crisis-recovery cycle, 60, 64
Curriculum materials, 27

Deviance:
  of children, 133
  teacher, 13, 32
Disclosure anxiety, 53, 71, 84

Empathic understanding, 30, 116,
  138-40

Feedback:
  from adults, 31
  from children, 27, 121-22
  giving of, 31
  receiving, 35
Follow-up study, teacher
  graduates, 11

Group approaches:
  analytic group discussion, 23
  as data collection, 26
  seminar and group
    psychoanalytic, 24
  to enhance use of self, 26-28
  psychoanalytic-
    interpretive, 23
  psychotherapeutically
    oriented, 24
Group process:
  as skill acquisition, 31-32
  experiental dimensions, 30
  objectives, 24
  outcome measures, 24
  phase sequence, 24
  preparation of teachers, 39-42
  training in group skills, 29-31
  training for interpersonal
    competence, 33, 36
Group-centered process, 34 (See
  also Sensitivity training;
  Laboratory training)

Also by Sharon Creech

Walk Two Moons
Absolutely Normal Chaos

Pleasing the Ghost